Whitley St. Helens Churchyard Hexhamshire

Headstones and Burials
May 1696 to January 2003

Dedicated to all Hexhamshire families
who have gone before

Whitley St. Helens Churchyard, Hexhamshire
Headstones and Burials May 1696 to January 2003

Compiled by Hilary Kristensen

Published by Wagtail Press

Designed and printed by
Shire Computer Services
e-mail: shirecs@hotmail.com

Bound by Jack Robinson & Son
Corbridge

Wagtail Press
Gairshield
Steel, Hexham
Northumberland
NE47 0HS
website: www.wagtailpress.co.uk
e-mail: enquiries@wagtailpress.co.uk

Wagtail Press
2003

ISBN 0-9538443-3-1

Acknowledgements

Local history research - Hilary Kristensen

Recording / transcribing of headstones in old churchyard-Hilary Kristensen, Bernard & Denise Baxter

Recording & plan of lower churchyard - Ulric Dixon

Photographs & sketches - Maureen Campbell

I would like to thank family and friends for all their help with deciphering and recording the headstone inscriptions in the old churchyard; it has been a very time - consuming but fascinating project. No burial plan has been traced so we had to start from scratch. In particular I would like to thank Bernard and Denise Baxter who have been enthusiastic transcribers from the start; without their help and encouragement it would have been difficult to complete the project. Thanks also to Maureen Campbell, Ann Porter and Catherine Wilson for their help and to Ulric Dixon who kindly allowed me to include his plan and details of the 'new' lower churchyard.

I am indebted to the Northumberland & Durham Family History Society, Hexham Library and Northumberland Records Office for their assistance with tracing parish records and burial registers.

Last, but definitely not least, I would like to thank everyone who helped clear and tidy up the overgrown areas of the old churchyard - In partiular the Whitley Chapel Young Farmers Club.

I have tried to be accurate with the recording of names, dates & details but please accept my apologies if mistakes have been made.

Contents

*Please note that spellings of names & places are as recorded from
headstones and burial registers*

Plan of Old Churchyard

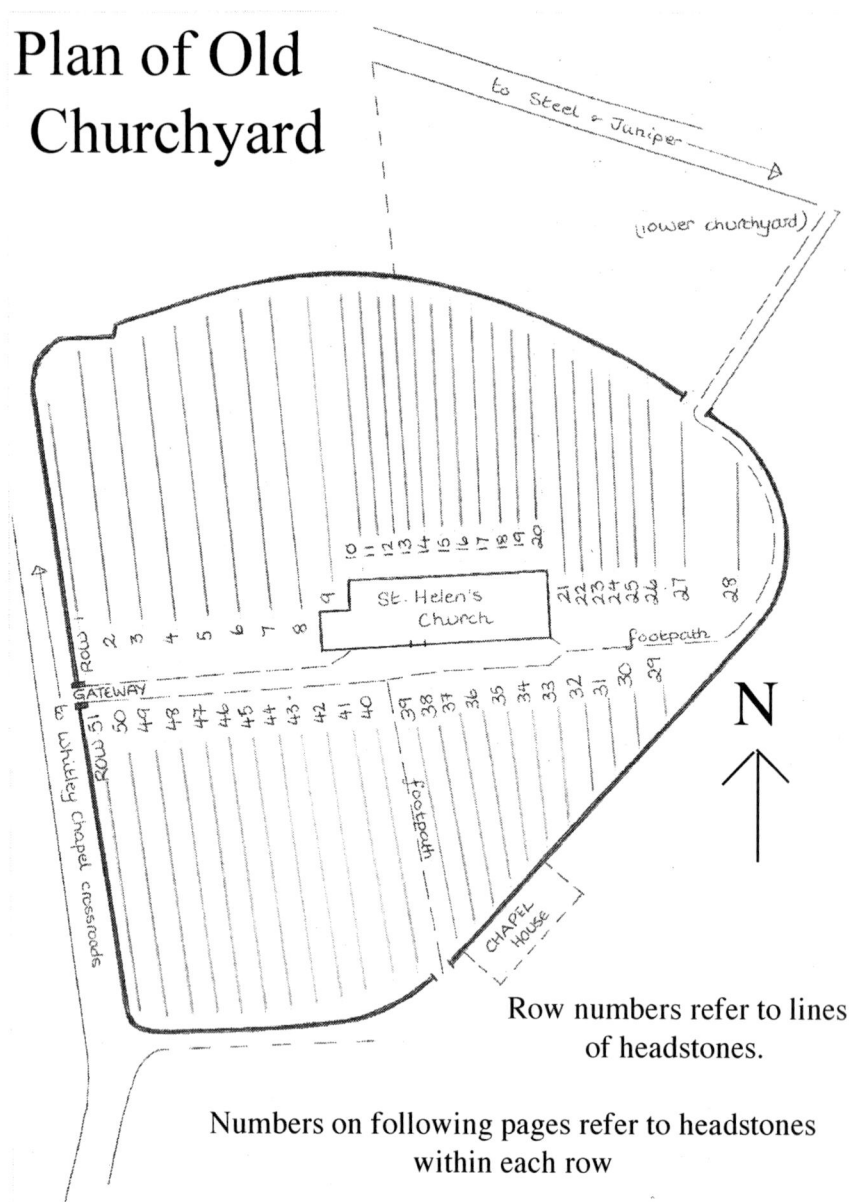

Row numbers refer to lines
of headstones.

Numbers on following pages refer to headstones
within each row

All rows start nearest to church.

TRANSCRIBED HEADSTONES IN OLD CHURCHYARD

Row 1

1. In loving memory of EDIE, beloved wife of Robert Little and mother of Adam, of Dinlabyre Newcastleton died 5th January 1967 aged 72 years. Also the above ROBERT LITTLE died 1st February 1978 aged 86 years. Also their son ADAM ROBERT dear husband of Ella died 29th April 2002 aged 79 years

2. In loving memory of GEORGE DAVIDSON beloved husband of Rebecca Little (late of Harwood Shield) who died at Hexham August 28th 1930 aged 73 years. Also the above REBECCA who died February 29th 1936 aged 76 years. "At rest"

3. Erected to the memory of HELEN daughter of Robert and Jane Little of Harewood Shield who died June 11th 1850 aged 21 months, also GEORGE DAVIDSON, their son who died June 24th 1855 aged 8 years, also AGNES their daughter who died August 17th 1855 aged 1 month, also MARY JANE their eldest daughter who died November 6th 1871 aged 27 years. Also JANE DAVIDSON wife of the above Robert Little who died May 23rd 1882 aged 65 years. Also DAVID their eldest son who died in Australia November 21st 1891 aged 47 years. Also HELEN their daughter who died December 22nd 1891 aged 38 and is buried at Lasswade. Also of the above ROBERT LITTLE who died December 5th 1892 aged 78 years

4. In memory of JOHN WHITE, who died at Middle Acton July 15th 1863 aged 30 years, also ANN wife of the above who died at Rowley Head January 3rd 1883 aged 45 years

5. *Top of headstone broken off. "JANE, daughter of Thomas Pigg of Rowley Head died October 7th 1849 aged 10 years". The remaining headstone reads:* EDWARD, his son, died May 12th 1856 aged 10 years. MARGARET LAIDLER the beloved wife of the above Thomas Pigg who died October 2nd 1881 aged 69 years, also JANE their daughter who died at Rowley Head August 1st 1882 aged 29 years. Also of the above THOMAS PIGG of Rowley Head who died September 11th 1884 aged 71 years. Also of JOSEPH their son who died at Aydon Shields June 10th 1906 aged 56 years

6. In affectionate remembrance of WILLIAM SISTERSON farmer who died at Newbiggin Hall February 7th 1856 aged 55 years, also WILLIAM SISTERSON son of the above who died at Great Whittington July 23rd 1883 aged 40 years interred in Halton Churchyard, also JOHN SISTERSON son of the above who died at Toddridge December 3rd 1884 aged 44 years interred in Halton Churchyard, also ELIZABETH SISTERSON widow of the first named William who died at Great Whittington October 10th 1886 aged 80 years. Also MATTHEW SISTERSON eldest son of William and Elizabeth Sisterson who died at Hexham August 8th 1902 aged 64 years

7. "*J*". Inscription on an urn within one corner reads: "In loving memory of EDWARD H TURNBULL died November 25th 1943"

8. Sacred to the memory of PRUDHOE dear husband of Amy Jewitt who died at Salmonfield January 1938

8A In memory of JOHN FORSTER of Dipton Mill who died May 31st 1876 aged 67 MARGARET eldest daughter of the above who died June 7th 1874 aged 36 years, CATHERINE third daughter who died June 13th 1884 aged 27 years, also of ANN his wife who died at Hexham April 12th 1897 aged 77 years

<u>Row 2</u>

9. In loving memory of GEORGE WILLIAM dearly beloved son of George and Gladys Reed of the Foggett died June 10th 1936 aged 8 years.

10. In affectionate memory of our dearly beloved only son JOHN (JACKIE) CHARLTON died 22 August 1943 aged 20 years *"Till we meet again"*

11. Stone vase inscribed DOROTHY

12. In loving memory of GEORGE ROBSON of Juniper Hexhamshire who died November 15th 1891 aged 71 years, also of MARY ELLEN his wife who died February 6th 1892 aged 57 years

8

13. In memory of THOMAS ANDERSON of Dipton Mill who died November 13th 1854 aged 78 years, also HANNAH wife of the above died May 6th 1854 aged 79 years, also RICHARD son of the above died November 26th 1842 aged 29 years. Also JOHN ANDERSON who died at Hole House June 16th 1896 aged 81 years, also MARY his wife who died at Hole House March 16th 1896 aged 68 years

14. In memory of MATTHEW WHITE of Westburnhope who died September 12th 1873 aged 75 years, also MARY his wife who died at Westburnhope May 18th 1883 aged 77 years

15. In memory of WILLIAM WALTON of Lamb Shield Mill who died July 1st 1867 aged 66 years, also of JANE his wife who died September 30th 1883 aged 81 years. Also of HANNAH HARRISON who died November 3rd 1879 aged 43 years

16. In remembrance of ISABELLA widow of William Taylor and eldest daughter of William and Jane Walton of Lambshield Mill who died at 13 Millfield Terrace Hexham October 8th 1926 in her 93rd year

17. In memory of RICHARD SCOTT who died at Walk Mill August 1st 1872 aged 19 years- *broken columnar headstone*

18. In memory of JANE the beloved wife of William Scott who died at Hall Barns Simonburn on the 17th day of March 1882 aged 67 years

19. In memory of JAMES son of William Scott who died at Hall Barns Simonburn on the 7th day of March 1882 aged 35 years

20. In loving memory of ARCHIBALD SCOTT Civil Engineer Public Works Department Simla Punjab India son of William Scott of Hall Barns Simonburn Northumberland who departed this life on May 12th 1890 aged 50 years and 10 months

> *"Now the labourer's task is o'er*
> *Now the battle-day is past*
> *Now upon the farther shore*
> *Lands the voyager at last*

Father in thy gracious keep
Leave we now thy servant sleep"

21. In loving memory of THOMAS HOOK who died at The Lee October 9th 1889 aged 88 years

<u>Row 4</u>

22. In memory of GORDON beloved child of Thomas and Eva Little who died on November 16th 1937 aged 3 years

23. Erected in memory of NICHOLAS STOBBS who died at Black Hall June 11th 1866 aged 89 years, also of MARGERY his wife who died March 6th 1868 aged 87 years

24. In memory of JANE wife of John Lamb of Lee Grange who died November 4th 1864 aged 42 years, also of DOROTHY their daughter who died January 4th 1872 aged 16 years. Also of the above JOHN LAMB who died at Cocker Letch April 28th 1897 aged 84 years

25. In affectionate remembrance of JOSEPH CHATT of Parker's House who died April 1st 1889 aged 84 years, also JANE wife of the above who died March 2nd 1886 aged 58 years

26. In loving memory of MARY FORSTER, February 21st 1890, aged 64 years: *inscribed on edge of circular flat stone*

27. In loving memory of JANE beloved wife of Ralph Pickering who died at Stobby Lea July 18th 1907 aged 69 years. Also of the above RALPH PICKERING who died at Long Lea February 6th 1915 aged 84 years

<u>Row 5</u>

28. In memory of JOHN THORNBURN who died at Foggat August 15th 1851 aged 57 years, also JOHN his son died February 8th 1855 aged 18 years, also JAMES his son died July 31st 1873 aged 31 years, also FRANCIS his son died November 11th 1877 aged 33 years, also RICHARD his son died January 12th 1878 aged 45 years. Also ANN wife of the above John who died February 10th 1888 aged 89 years

10

29. In loving memory of ANDREW THORBURN of Foggott Farm who died June 9th 1902 aged 68 years

Row 6

30. In loving memory of RICHARD THORBURN, The Holmes Hexhamshire who died (the result of an accident) 12th January 1878 aged 45 years, also of MARGARET, his wife who died 1st March 1913 aged 82 years, also of JOHN WILLIAM, son of the above who died 22nd July 1917 aged 48 years. *"At rest"*

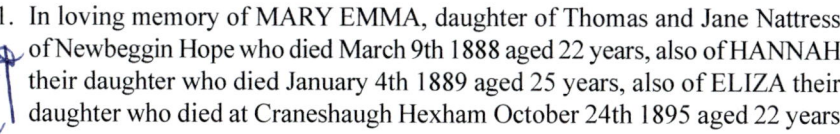

31. In loving memory of MARY EMMA, daughter of Thomas and Jane Nattress of Newbeggin Hope who died March 9th 1888 aged 22 years, also of HANNAH their daughter who died January 4th 1889 aged 25 years, also of ELIZA their daughter who died at Craneshaugh Hexham October 24th 1895 aged 22 years

Row 7

32. In loving memory of WILLIAM DODD of Hamburn Hall who died May 4th 1869 aged 84 years, also of SARAH his wife who died March 18th 1867 aged 71 years, also of JOSEPH their eldest son who died January 16th 1890 aged 74 years, also of THOMAS their son who died January 19th 1901 aged 72 years, also of SARAH their daughter who died June 16th 1905 aged 72 years. And of ISAAC DODD died November 11th 1919 and RUTH his wife died April 13th 1920 both in their 84th year interred in Blackpool

33. In affectionate remembrance of THOMAS HALL who died at Lillswood January 10th 1877 aged 75 years, also of SUSANNAH his wife who died September 3rd 1878 aged 69 years, also ELIZABETH daughter of the above who died March 21st 1884 aged 30 years, also THOMAS son of the above who died November 2nd 1888 aged 52 years

34. In loving remembrance of MARY wife of Cuthbert Symn of Peth Foot who died January 23rd 1888 aged 63 years, also WILLIAM their eldest son who died January 18th 1867 aged 22 years. Also the above CUTHBERT SYMN who died July 13th 1907 aged 85 years. Also JOHN their son who died October 31st 1907 aged 60 years

11

35. In loving memory of MARY ANN wife of Matthew Cowing of Embley who died February 1st 1898 aged 63 years. Also of the above MATTHEW COWING who died June 10th 1918 aged 86 years. Also ABRAM their son who died May 13th 1895 aged 20 years, also ISABELL their daughter who died June 13th 1897 aged 33 years, also FRANCES their daughter wife of John Dinning of Benwell who died July 9th 1893 aged 32 years, also GEORGE ANTHONY COWING their son who died July 4th 1937 aged 66 years. Also MILDRED COWING who died June 1st 1938 aged 69 years

Row 8

36. In memory of ROBERT ERRINGTON of High Eardley who died the 15th April 1795 aged 74 years

37. In memory of MARY wife of Andrew Thorburn of Mire House who died 25th December 1830 aged 69 years, also of the above ANDREW THORBURN who died 6th September 1853 aged 92 years. Also of HANNAH wife of William Allcroft of Slaley and daughter of the above who died 14th July 1868 aged 66 years. Also of the above WILLIAM ALLCROFT who died January 9th 1879 aged 82 years. Also of JAMES THORBURN who died April 9th 1881 aged 72 years

38. In loving memory of WILLIAM DODD of Channel Well who died April 3rd 1898 aged 62 years, also ANNE his wife who died January 19th 1900 aged 64 years, also MARY their daughter who died at Ordley July 16th 1892 aged 28 years, also THOMAS their son who died August 10th 1935 aged 65 years, and of JAMES their son who died at Channel Well January 25th 1951 aged 74 years. Also FRANCES his wife who died January 23rd 1943 aged 70 years. Also EVELYN MARY their daughter who died September 30th 1915 aged 3 years

Row 9

39. In loving memory of JOHN ERRINGTON who died at Dukesfield Hall Slaley July 26th 1899 in his 60th year

40. Sacred to the memory of ROBERT ERRINGTON dearly beloved husband of Isabella Errington of Grovy Field departed this life May 5th 1814 in the 35th year of his age.

inscription on rear of stone: "Died in faithfull hope of a blessed resurrection. The Lord giveth and the Lord taketh away. Blessed be the name of the Lord"

41. Here lies the body of MARY daughter of Richard Errington of Mire House who died March 7th 1797 aged 19 years ?, also his son THOMAS died April 22nd 1803 aged 12 years

42. In loving memory of THOMAS FOSTER ERRINGTON of Wood Hall who died March 3rd 1898 aged 61 years, also of HANNAH wife of the above who died at Hexham March 15th 1921 aged 86 years

43. In memory of ANTHONY eldest son of William and Jane Cook who died at The Holmes October 15th 1849 aged 3 years and 4 months, also GEORGE CARR their 5th son who died August 25th 1863 aged 5 months, also EMILY their youngest daughter who died May 30th 1864 aged 2 years and 10 months, also ANTHONY their third son who died March 24th 1875 aged 24 years, also CICELY their third daughter born November 8th 1847 died November 1st 1895, also WILLIAM their second son born May 8th 1849 died May 30th 1896. Also JANE COOK mother of the above who died at Hexham May 5th 1899 aged 79 years, also WILLIAM COOK husband of the above who died January 10th 1900 aged 78 years, also MARGERY their daughter who died September 27th 1916 aged 60 years

    inscription on back of headstone:
    "As the winged arrow flies
    Swift its destined mark to find
    As the lightning from the skies
    Darts and leaves no trace behind
    Thus with speed our fleeting days
    Bear us down life's rapid stream
    Lord on high our wishes raise
    All on earth is but a dream"

44. In loving memory of MARGARET JANE, daughter of the late William and Jane Cook who died November 2nd 1934 in her 90th year, also THOMAS DIXON M.B.C.M. their fourth son who died at Torquay August 4th and was interred in Torquay cemetery August 8th 1940 aged 81 years, also JANE their daughter who died August 19th 1946 aged 92 years

45. In affectionate remembrance of GEORGE OLIVER of Dotland who died October 26th 1878 aged 83 years, also of MARY his wife who died at Newbiggin July 15th 1853 aged 57 years and was interred at Hunstonworth Church, also of GEORGE OLIVER of Dotland son of the above who died on the 13th November 1889 aged 67 years, also of JOHN BELL OLIVER of Dotland son of the above who died on the 7th of November 1884 aged 25 years, also of MARY wife of the above George Oliver who died at Leazes Head December 28th 1907 aged 78 years

46. In loving memory of MARY HANNAH beloved wife of Thomas Robson who departed this life at Lowgate 4th February 1912 aged 29 years, also of the above THOMAS ROBSON who died at Newcastle Infirmary September 30th 1915 aged 32 years

47. In loving memory of WILLIAM PAUL of White Hall who died September 17th 1910 aged 68 years, also DOROTHY his wife who died February 18th 1898 aged 50 years, also MARY ANN HARBOTTLE mother of the above who died October 12th 1902 aged 81 years

48. In loving memory of JOHN BELL late schoolmaster Lilswood who died at Broadwell House 24th April 1910 aged 72 years, also of ELIZABETH his wife who died at Broadwell House 22nd August 1910 aged 70 years

49. In loving memory of MARY wife of John Robson of Whitehall who died March 4th 1904 aged 76 years, also the above JOHN who died July 16th 1908 aged 74 years, also of their daughter ISABELLA who died November 16th 1918 aged 54 years

50. In loving memory of MARY JANE beloved child of Isabella Robson who died at Whitehall April 17th 1896 aged 6 years. *"Not lost just gone before"*

51. In loving memory of SARAH PICKERING of Eads Bush Hexhamshire who died 27th May 1916 aged 73 years, also WILLIAM PICKERING who died at Eads Bush 21st February 1917 aged 76 years, also JOSEPH PICKERING who died at Eads Bush 7th June 1919 aged 70 years

52. In loving memory of ANN wife of Andrew Laing who died at Hesleywell Hexhamshire May 31st 1905 aged 73 years, also the above ANDREW who died at Hexham November 30th 1907 aged 73 years

Row 10

53. In loving memory of ELLEN MARSHALL wife of Bennet Marshall who departed this life July 31st 1903 at Lee Moor Houses aged 77 years, also of GEORGE CUMMINGS brother of the above who died at The Palms December 1st 1884 aged 71 years. Also of ANTHONY FORSTER CHARLTON beloved husband of Dorothy Charlton of Dye House who died December 10th 1918 aged 36 years, and of ANTHONY ELLIOT CHARLTON son of the above who died April 8th 1918 aged 7 months

54. In loving memory of ELIZABETH KIRSOPP of Loaning House who died 27th April 1933 aged 66 years

Row 11

55. In loving memory of a dear wife MARGERY RODDAM of Dye House Steel Hexham died 18th February 1992 aged 65 years

56. LAURA CROSS late of Dotland Grange who died 28th June 1991. Dearly loved   *RIP*

57. JACK BRIAN CROSS of Dotland Grange who died 20th April 1981. Dearly loved   *RIP*

58. In loving memory of ADA beloved wife of Fred J Moralee of Low Ardley who died February 3rd 1920 in her 42nd year, also the above FRED J MORALEE who died December 18th 1952 in his 73rd year *"Thy will be done"*

59. In loving memory of JOHN BOLAM of Hesleywell who died February 20th 1874 aged 84 years, also JANE wife of the above who died March 30th 1869 aged 87 years. Also ALLXANDER PATRICK who died at Hesley Well June 7th 1868 aged 38 years, also ANNIE his wife and daughter of the above John Bolam who died at No. 4 Commercial Place Hexham January 8th 1890 aged 49 years

60. In loving memory of EPHRAIM HEDLEY of Low Ardley who died July 13th 1882 aged 64 years, also ELEANOR his wife who died April 15th 1897 aged 65 years, also ELIZABETH CATHERINE their daughter who

died November 11th 1934 aged 76 years, also JOSEPH their son who died February 13th 1937 aged 74 years, also JOHN their son who died October 19th 1937 aged 77 years

61. JOHN DINNING who died at Houtley May 12th 1891 aged 57 years, also of MARGARET and JAMES children of the above who died in infancy, also ANN wife of the above John Dinning who died November 8th 1907 aged 64 years, also JANE their daughter who died June 30th 1921 aged 51 years, MARGERY died February 18th 1941 aged 79 years, THOMASIN ANN died June 30th 1941 aged 73 years

62. In loving memory of MARGARET H MAUGHAN who died at Lord's Lot Farm December 3rd 1902 aged 59 years, also WILLIAM her husband who died October 1st 1923 aged 80 years *"They rest from their labours"*

63. In loving memory of SAMUEL CARR who died 11th May 1932 aged 69 years, also of SARAH beloved wife of the above who died 28th January 1940 aged 77 years, also FLORENCE ELLENOR daughter of the above who died 21st October 1919 aged 17 years, also JOHN HENRY infant son of the above who died 11th April 1886

Row 12

64. In loving memory of THOMAS NICHOL of Turf House who died 3rd July 1888 aged 91 years, also of HANNAH his wife who died 9th July 1889 aged 85 years, also SAMUEL NICHOL their son who died 21st July 1919 aged 79 years, also SARAH his wife who died 27th October 1881 aged 32 years, also MARY ELIZABETH their daughter who died 7th September 1878 aged 7 months, and of MARY his wife who died 23rd June 1899 aged 39 years

65. JOAN ROSS 1932 - 1984 *"I know that thy redeemer liveth"*

66. In loving memory of RICHARD TWEDDLE who died at Raw Green 7th February 1882 aged 63 years, RICHARD second son died May 26th 1849 aged 3 weeks, JOHN eldest son died September 12th 1853 aged 6 1/2 years, ALICE JANE second daughter died June 20th 1878 aged 23 years. Also ALICE JANE dearly beloved wife of the above who died at East Gate

Hexham October 6th 1897 aged 74 years, also HANNAH FRANCIS youngest daughter of the above who died at Shield Close Farm Hexham November 5th 1915 aged 51 years interred at Hexham cemetery

67. In loving memory of JOSEPH FAIRLESS of Spittal Shield who died November 22nd aged 68 years, also MARY his wife died at Sinderhope Shield Allendale May 28th 1910 aged 80 years

68. In loving memory of ANNIE ELLEN COMMON who died at Park House December 8th 1920 aged 37 years, also MARY ANN dearly beloved wife of James Common who died at Park House June 14th 1924 aged 65 years, also the above JAMES who died March 11th 1930 aged 75 years

Row 13

69. *"DLI 8th Battalion"* To the memory of JOHN ANGUS LEYBOURNE of Nunsbrough Ordley born 31 August 1919 died 28th January 1985

70. In affectionate remembrance of JAMES NEILSON who died at Mire Meadows September 28th 1881 aged 42 years, also HANNAH, daughter of the above who died May 16th 1889 aged 17 years, also ALEXANDER son of the above who died November 20th 1889 aged 24 years, also MARY JANE daughter of the above died September 25th 1892 aged 23 years. Also ANN ELLEN daughter of James Nielson, wife of Michael James Winter died at Mire Meadows June 6th 1905 aged 42 years. Also HANNAH wife of the above James Nielson who died at Earthley Mires October 26th 1911 aged 72 years

71. In loving memory of W GORDON CAMPBELL 1922-2000. Dear husband of Maureen

Row 14

72. In loving memory of MARGARET wife of Joseph Dixon of Close House who died June 10th 1894 ged 76 years *["Asleep in Jesus"]*. The above JOSEPH DIXON who died September 20th 1898 aged 82 years. Also JOSEPH their son died died February 27th 1898 aged 51 years

73. *"Take ye heed watch and pray forgive."* In memory of WILLIAM STOKOE of Raw Green who died November 25th 1884 aged 79 years, also ANN wife of the above who died at Mire Meadows June 25th 1892 aged 78 years

17

74. In loving memory of RALPH PATRICK who died at Grouse House Hexhamshire 6th September 1924 aged 60 years, also THOMASINA MARGARET, wife of the above, who died 25th April 1944 aged 75 years

75. In loving memory of ROBERT JAMES TURNBULL of Litharge Hexhamshire who died April 14th 1926 aged 64 years, also HANNAH wife of the above who died June 18th 1948 in her 77th year. Also of HANNAH TURNBULL sister of the above who died June 24th 1927 aged 60 years. Also of JOHN TURNBULL father of the above who died April 21st 1868 aged 63 years

Row 15

76. In loving memory of MICHAEL BELL who died at Low Raw Green January 2nd 1909 aged 47 years, also of ANNIE his wife who died 21st April 1956 aged 89 years, also of REBECCA daughter of the above died 4th January 1923 aged 28 years

77. In loving memory of MATTHEW HENRY husband of Meggie Clark of Gunnerton Fell who died April 7th 1940 aged 47 years, also the above MEGGIE CLARK died January 13th 1951 aged 65 years

78. In loving memory of MARY ANN wife of William Clark who died at Stotsfold Lodge April 25th 1933 aged 72 years, also WILLIAM CLARK who died January 25th 1942 aged 82 years, also THOMAS NIXON son of the above who died at Dye House June 18th 1893 aged 3 years

79. In loving memory of JOHN REAY of Juniper who died 14th March 1953 aged 77 years, also CATHERINE wife of the above who died 3rd February 1933 aged 53 years

80. JOSEPH LISHMAN 1868 - 1939

Row 16

81. In loving remembrance of THOMAS WILLIAM LITTLE who died 29th September 1948 aged 27 years *Two vases stand in front of the headstone: "In loving memory" and "In loving memory of MARGARET HALL died October 7th 1941"*

18

Row 17

82. In loving memory of EDWARD DALTON STOBBS of High Dalton who died September 29th 1949 aged 66 years, also CATHERINE his dear wife who died April 22nd 1975 aged 89 years

83. In loving memory of THOMAS MOORE late of Oakerlands who died November 21st 1922 aged 80 years, also JANE ANN his beloved wife who died October 21st 1934 aged 71 years

84. *A sundial with "Sweet is the fragrance of remembrance" carved on three sides of the dial table; carved on two kerbstones forming the western edge of the plot is.* ROBERT ANDERSON BALDERSTON died 12th June 1958 aged 54 *and* ROBERT COWEN STOWELL born 18th March 1906 died 14th January 1933

85. GEORGE CHARLTON son of George Alexander and Florence Ada Connell Kitty Frisk Hexham died August 27th 1927 in his 23rd year

86. In loving memory of my dear husband THOMAS WILLIAM ARMSTRONG who died at Swallowship Cottage April 22nd 1948 aged 68 years. Also GRACE his dear wife who died 28th December 1963 aged 87 years. Their dear son Cpl FRED ARMSTRONG killed in action at Knightsbridge May 27th 1942 aged 23 years. *"At peace"*

87. DAVID JOHN dearly beloved husband of Isabella Harkness fell asleep December14th 1932 in his 31st year

Row 18

88. In loving memory of ANN ATKINSON born 1840 died 1928

89. In loving memory of JOSEPH NEVIN dearly beloved husband of Mary A Reed of High Eshells who died April 11th 1929 aged 60 years. MARY ANN REED who died February 8th 1971 aged 96 years. Also of their eldest son JOSEPH WILLIAM born 3rd December 1906 died 5th December 1906. Also ISAAC their son who died October 2nd 1940 aged 28 years

90. In loving memory of our dear parents JOHN ARMSTRONG who died 8th November 1942 aged 55 years and BARBARA JANE ARMSTRONG who died 1st April 1976 aged 84 years

91. In loving memory of SARAH wife of William Watson who died 27th January 1948 aged 66 years. GEORGE son of the above who died 25th March 1933 aged 23 years. WILLIAM husband of Sarah who died January 23rd 1951 aged 72 years

92. In loving memory of THOMAS WHITE who died at Mire Meadows 3rd May 1921 aged 80 years, also ANNIE wife of the above who died 23rd December 1953 aged 87 years

Row 19

93. In loving memory of MATTHEW HENRY son of William and Jane White who died at Low Staples July 15th 1880 aged 14 years, also THOMAS SIDNEY their son who died May 19th 1886 aged 15 years. Also the above WILLIAM who died December 14th 1908 aged 73 years. Also JOHN WILLIAM their son who died September 16th 1924 aged 55 years. Also the above JANE WHITE who died February 4th 1926 aged 84 years. Also infant daughter of A and J White who died December 2nd 1924. Also ARTHUR LEONARD their son who died May 21st 1965 aged 92 years

94. In loving memory of LILLIAN wife of John Atkinson and daughter of W and J White of Low Staples who died 23rd June 1957 aged 90 years. Also the above JOHN ATKINSON who died 28th March 1935 aged 64 years interred at Newburn

Row 20

95. DOROTHY ANN, daughter of William and Dorothy Anderson of Hollybush Close, who died February 1st 1861 aged 15 months, JOHN ROBSON, their son, died February 4th 1861 aged 3 years, JOHN GEORGE, their son, died May 30th 1866 aged 13 months, WILLIAM ANDERSON died December 21st 1870 aged 52 years, DOROTHY, daughter of the above, died July 13th 1883 aged 16 years, LANCELOT, their son, who died October 17th 1890 aged 25 years, also William, their son, who died October 5th 1890 aged 20 years. DOROTHY ANDERSON, wife of the above, died February 20th 1910 aged 80 years

96. MARY ELLEN, wife of Robert Blackett Charlton, The Linnels, Hexhamshire died 10th July 1920 aged 66 years, ROBERT BLACKETT, husband of Mary Ellen Charlton, died 15th June 1953 aged 101 years and 9 months, FLORENCE ADA CONNELL, wife of George Alexander Connell and daughter of Robert and Mary Charlton, died 4th February 1961 in her 87th years

97. In Loving Memory of NICHOLAS SPARKE BATEY of Dipton Mill fell asleep 5th January 1938 aged 60 years, and his beloved wife ISABELL BATEY passed away 10th September 1939 aged 69 years *"At rest"*

98. In Loving Memory of THOMAS URWIN who died 15th June 1938 aged 57 years. Also ISABELLA MARGARET, his wife, who died 6th March 1937 aged 54 years

99. In Loving Memory of GEORGE ANTHONY DIXON of Hexham who passed away 30th August 1937 in his 79th years

Row 21

100. JANE YARROW, the beloved wife of George Watson of Riding Hills, who died April 6th 1890 aged 56 years, PEARSON PRINGLE, son of the above, who died January 21st 1879 aged 19 years, GEORGE BELL, their son, who died August 1st 1881 aged 19 years, JOHN, their son, who died February 29th 1892 aged 26 years, ARTHUR, their son, who died in Port Jinja B.E. Africa June 14th 1906 aged 36 years, GEORGE WATSON of Riding Hills who died April 14th 1909 aged 72 years

101. Here lies all that was mortal of THE REVEREND ABRAHAM BROWN upwards of 60 years Minister of Whitley Chapel and its first Perpetual Curate who died November 8th 1812 aged 92 years, also of ALICE his wife who died January 6th 1780

102. In memory of ROBERT BELL of Mollersteads who died December 13th 1873 aged 51 years, MARY ANN, wife of the above, who died at Earthly Mires January 2nd 1902 aged 74 years, ELIZABETH, daughter of the above, who died December 4th 1859 aged 10 years, HANNAH, daughter of the above, who died December 31st 1876 aged 19 years, ELIZABETH, wife of Thomas Forster, and daughter of the above who died at Mollersteads April 30th 1899 aged 31 years

103. In memory of ROBERT I. ARMSTRONG, born at Ettleton February 14th 1827, died at Gairshield August 8th 1912

104. DOUGLAS? FORREST died 1893 aged ? years

105. In loving memory of WILLIAM ANDERSON FORREST who died at Peth Foot March 13th 1896 aged 14 years, also of JOHN CHRISTOPHER FORREST who died August 21st 1895 aged 3 months

Row 22

106. In memory of my late dear husband JOHN CURRY of Gairshield who died December 31st 1773, 57 years. This monumental tombstone was erected by his affectionate and afflicted widow Mildred C. MILDRED CURRY, wife of John Curry, died June 2nd 1797 aged 79. *On reverse of stone:* In memory of MATTHEW, son of John Curry, died June 20th 1784 et 32 ?, THOMAS, son of John Curry, who died May 11th 1790 aged ?

107. In loving memory of JOHN ROBSON of Pasture House who died 8th May 1938 aged 61 years, GEORGE WILLIAM ROBSON, brother of above, who died 7th April 1942 aged 61 years

Row 23

108. In loving Memory of HENRY ROBSON who died at Windy Hill August 1938 aged 80 years, also FRANCES JANE, his wife, who died March 1936 aged 67 years, also HENRY, their son and husband of Margaret Robson, who died August 1935 aged 41 years, also FRANCES EVELYN, their daughter and wife of William Heron, who died at Shield Green July 1939 aged 42 years, also WILLIAM HERON died April 1969 aged 86 years, also ANNIE ALICE, their daughter and dear wife of Edward Harding, who died 27th May 1968 aged 63 years

Row 24

109. In memory of ROBERT CHARLTON BIRKS, who died November 24th 1824 aged 84 years, also ELIZABETH, wife of the above, died June 2nd

110. In affectionate remembrance of ROBERT CHARLTON who died at Ordley
June 23rd 1843 aged 62 years, also MARY, daughter of the above, who died
May 14th 1884 aged 52 years, also ELIZABETH, daughter of the above,
who died February 24th 1885 aged 54 years, also ANN CHARLTON, wife
of the above, who died February 3rd 1899 aged 90 years, also ROBERT
CHARLTON, their son, who died August 21st 1898 aged 61 years

111. MOLLIE CORBY 1904 - 1980

Row 25

112. The burial place of JOHN FEATHERSTON of Blackhall in this county who
died 4th October 1808 aged 70 years, also BARBARA relict of the above
who died 3rd July 1821 aged 71 years and three of their children,
MARGARET, WHARTON, and THOMAS who died at different periods of
time

113. *Headstone lying flat over grave in front of above (112) which seems to be a
replacement for this* JOHN FEATHERSTON late of Blackhall 4th October
1808 aged 70 years, also MARGARET, his daughter, died February 13th
1780., also WHARTON died 22nd August 1787 aged 3 weeks, also
BARBARA, his widow, who died the 3rd day of July 1821 aged 71 years

114. *No headstone, only plain kerbs, bodystone missing, nothing recorded, very
poor condition*

115. In loving memory of CLARENCE DALRYMPLE SMITH born May 16th
1868 died February 3rd 1941, and CICELY SMITH born October 24th 1881
died September 22nd 1952

116. EDWARD HARDING died 23rd February 1935 aged 63 years, also
MARGARET his dear wife died 13th June 1935 aged 60 years, late of
Dalton

Row 26

117. In loving memory of the Rev WILLIAM SISSON for 65 years Vicar of this
parish, and for 52 years Vicar of Slaley and St. Helens combined. Born at
Orton Westmoreland June 2nd 1816 died at Slaley Vicarage July 17th 1906

118. In memory of ELIZABETH, the beloved wife, of William Sisson, Vicar of St. Helens with Slaley. Born Dinning at Dukesfield Hall November 29th 1824 died at the parsonage Slaley May 20th 1876. *"Blessed everyone that feareth the Lord, that walketh in his way"*

Row 27

119. In memory of SARAH HANNAH KENNEDY, loving wife of Henry who died 1st November 1982 aged 76 years

120. Treasured memories of HENRY, dear husband of Sarah Hannah Kennedy, who died 8th November 1958 aged 67 years *"Sweet are the memories, silently kept of one I loved dearly and will never forget*

121. In loving memory of AGNES DAGG, beloved wife of William Kennedy, who died at Eads Bush 24th November 1932 aged 72 years, also the above WILLIAM who died at Eads Bush 9th December 1941 in his 80th year, also WILLIAM, their son, killed in action at Loos, France 10th October 1917 in his 20th year

122. In loving memory of MARGARET ANNIE, beloved wife of Henry Kennedy, who died at Burn Shield Haugh 10th September 1932 aged 38 years

123. In loving memory of BETTY, beloved daughter of John and Olive Kennedy, who died Hawkhope Hill, Falstone December 1937 aged 16 years. *"Rest in peace"*

Row 28

124. JOHN TELFER 1850 - 1930, MARGARET ANN TELFER 1840 - 1940, LIZZIE TELFER 1880 - 1908

125. In loving memory of WILLIAM HOGARTH who died June 6th 1860 aged 61 years, WILLIAM, his son, died May 12th 1835 aged 6 years, also ANN, his beloved wife, died October 28th 1873 aged 78 years, also ROBERT HOGARTH who died September 24th 1910 aged 71 years, also MARGARET, his wife, who died June 29th 1891 aged 41 years

126. In memory of ANTHONY JOHNSON of High Ardley who died June 17th
1891 aged 74 years, also ANN beloved wife of the above who died February
17th 1911 aged 72 years, also GEORGE JOHNSON their son who died July
30th 1900 aged 36 years

127. In loving memory of WILLIAM ANGUS of Salmon Field, Hexhamshire
who died August 14th 1806 aged 62 years, also of ISABELLA his wife who
died December 20th 1913 aged 70 years

128. In loving memory of ELIZABETH daughter of Thomas and Margaret Dixon
of Tenter House who died August 26th 1893 aged 7 years and 5 months, also
the above MARGARET DIXON who died May 2nd 1911 aged 69 years,
also the above THOMAS DIXON who died October 26th 1921 aged 81
years, also MARY second daughter of the above who died February 4th
1933 aged 60 years

Row 30

129. In memory of WILLIAM son of John Dixon of Juniper who died October
15th 1837 aged 28 years, also HANNAH wife of the above John Dixon died
December 15th 1847 aged 74 years, also the above JOHN DIXON who died
July 27th 1854 aged 80 years, also JOHN his son died August 10th 1866
aged 62 years

130. In memory of JOHN RICHARDSON and DOROTHY of Ordley Hall. She
died 2nd ? of February 1792 aged 50. He died 21st of July 1795 aged 66

131. In memory of THOMAS BRISCOE of Ordley who departed this life July
25th 1825 aged 65 years

Row 31

132. The burial place of WILLIAM CURREY Lilswood, ANN BELL his
daughter died December 12th 1812 aged 33 years, the above WILLIAM
CURREY departed this life June 10th 1814 aged 62 years, also
MARGARET his wife who died April 25th 1837 aged 85 years,

also ROBERT their son who died at Longlee July 5th 1851 aged 54 years, also MILDRED DODD their daughter who died at High Staples February 4th 1847 aged 55 years, also JAMES DODD her husband died 25th February 1870 aged 80 years

133. In memory of MICHAEL DODD Black Hall who died May 3rd 1859 aged 73 years, also MARY his wife who died at Morton Grange January 31st 1873 aged 77 years, also MARGARET their daughter who died February 11th 1848 aged 28 years, also ELEANOR wife of William Dodd of Black Hall who died April 26th 1861 aged 33 years, also the above WILLIAM DODD of East Benton who died September 1st 1890 aged 66 years, also THOMASIN widow of the above William Dodd who died March 1st 1895 in her 74th year

134. In loving memory of THOMAS DODD who died at The Riding St. Johns Lee May 24th 1882 aged 62 years, also THOMAS son of the above who died at Dye House February 20th 1870 aged 15 years, also MARY wife of the above Thomas Dodd who died at Low Warden September 3rd 1893 aged 73 years, also JOHN son of the above who died at Whinetley February 12th 1906 aged 58 years, also GEORGE CHARLTON son of the above John Dodd who died in infancy, also FRANCES wife of the above John who died at 5 Leazes Crescent Hexham November 8th 1934 aged 82 years

135. In loving memory of JOHN THOMAS DODD who died at Prior House Haydon Bridge 12th November 1918 aged 30 years *"Peace perfect peace"*

Row 32

136. In memory of JOSHUA son of Edward Steel ob January 15th 1772 et 16 years, EDWARD STEEL ob August 12th 1781 et 59 years, FRANCES wife of Edward Steel died January 30th 1799 aged 80. *On the reverse:* In memory of JANE wife of Richard Fairlamb ob June 24th 1788 etat 36

137. GEORGE WHITE late of Steel died October 1st 1775 aged 79 years and MARY his wife died December 31st 1776 aged 74 years

138. In memory of ELIZABETH wife of John Leathard of the Steel who died 11th April 1800 aged 25 years

139. In loving memory of JOSEPH WANLACE of Newbiggin who died July
8th 1888 aged 76 years, also SARAH his daughter who died June 23rd
1860 aged 6 years and 9 months, also JANE his wife who died October
12th 1907 aged 83 years, also JOHN their son who died May 31st 1907
aged 49 years. Jane and John interred in North Gosforth cemetery. Also
LANCELOT WANLACE his brother who served 24 years in the 1st
Royal Dragoons and died at Newbiggin July 23rd 1861 aged 49 years

140. Here lies the body of BARBARA wife of Thomas Artley late of Ordley
May 4th 1776. THOMAS ARTLEY died 1784 aged 69 years

141. WILLIAM son of John and Jane Reed of Dotland died 25th October
1770 aged 16 years, ROBERT son of John and Jane Reed died 3rd
October 1772 aged 16 years

> *on reverse: "Youth and Virtue by death*
> *is not regarded*
> *but in the next world*
> *true virtues rewarded"*

Row 34

142. In loving memory of WILLIAM BELL of Aydon Shields Hexhamshire
who died at Whitley Bay May 11th 1902 aged 62 years, ELIZABETH
wife of the above who died at Whitley Bay November 4th 1923 aged 85
years, JOHN only son of the above who died December 12th 1871 aged
1 year, CATHERINE third daughter of the above who died January 17th
1919 aged 46 years, ELIZABETH their daughter who died December
7th 1960 aged 86 years, SARAH JANE their daughter who died
December 17th 1960 aged 80 years

143. Sacred to the memory of ELIZABETH wife of John Bell of Aydon
Shields who died January 18th 1836 in the 42nd year of age, JOHN
BELL who died at Aydon Shields December 11th 1868 aged 78 years,
ANN OLIVER only daughter of the above at Dotland September 5th
1863 aged 35 years, HANNAH widow of the above John Bell who died
at Aydon Shields May 25th 1896 aged 86 years

144. In memory of ROBERT DIXON of Mollersteads who died on 13th April 1832 aged 73 years, ANN his wife who died on 13th June 1837 aged 79 years, HANNAH SOPPITT their daughter who died on 26th January 1830 aged 31 years

145. HANNAH wife of Edward Dixon of Mollersteads born in March 1736 died October 7th 1765, EDWARD DIXON died January 9th 180(?) aged 7(?) years

146. HENRY DIXON late of Upper Stapple ob May 1st Anno Aetatis 74 Domini 1770, MARGARET wife of James Hudspith died October 19th 1848 aged 40 years

147. In memory of JOSEPH DIXON of Low Staples who died April 6th 1812 aged 81 years, also MARY his wife died November 21st 1824 aged 86 years, also ISABELLA wife of Peter Dixon died August 26th 1830 aged 46 years, also the above PETER DIXON died March 27th 1841 aged 70 years, also ANN DIXON daughter of the above Isabella and Peter Dixon died May 26th 1841 aged 20 years, also ISABELLA their daughter died November 7th 1859 aged 34 years

148. In Affectionate Remembrance, THOMAS son of Thomas and Ann Simpson Black Hall Mill who died May 1st 1866 aged 6 years, JOHN WHITE their son who died March 12th 1874 aged 4 years, ANNIE URSULA their daughter who died March 14th 1874 aged 1 year and 5 months, THOMAS SIMPSON who died March 24th 1888 aged 66 years, ANN SIMPSON beloved wife of the above who died October 22nd 1905 aged 74 years, CHRISTOPHER son of the above who died November 10th 1903 aged 42 years. *On back of stone:* In memory of CHRISTOPHER SIMPSON of Black Hall Mill, who died February 27th 1853 aged 80 years, JANE his beloved wife who died April 23rd 1877 aged 93 years

<u>Row 35</u>

149. Here lieth the body of ANNE wife of Edward Tinlin late of High Dalton who died April 18th 1771

150. In memory of EDWARD DIXON of Earthly Mires who died on 19th March 1865 aged 75 years, also of MARGARET wife of the above who died on 25th December 1858 aged 63 years

28

151. Here lies the body of WILLIAM ARMSTRONG of Park House who died December 4th 1768 aged 40, ELIZABETH his daughter died May 20th 1786 aged 40, also his wife ELIZABETH died July 19th 1792 aged 65

152. The burial place of GEORGE LINSLEY Fen House, clerk, at Whitley Chapel who died May 29th 1816 aged 51 years

153. In loving memory of WILLIAM OLIVER late of High Eshells who died April 14th 1914 aged 76 years, also of HANNAH HELEN his wife who died November 10th 1911 aged 68 years, also of HANNAH HELEN fourth daughter of the above died August 12th 1917 aged 42 years

154. Here lies the body of PERCIVAL DIXON son of Bell Dixon of Dukesfield who died February 4th 1811 aged 32 years, also of BELL his son who died July 14th 1813 aged 20 years

Row 37

155. In memory of WILLIAM JOHNSON of Newcastle on Tyne who died November 12th 1875 aged 86 years

156. In memory of MARY HANNAH wife of John Johnson of Dotland Park who died 28th June 1950 aged 81 years, JOHN JOHNSON who died 9th February 1963 aged 91 years

157. In loving memory of ANGUS PICKWORTH 1931 - 1982

158. The family burial place of JOHN and MARY JOHNSON of Hamburn Hall *"Lord, thou hast been our refuge, from one generation to another",* WILLIAM their youngest and last surviving son born April 20th 1790

159. JOHN JOHNSON of White Hall departed this life June 28th 1780 aged 82 years

160. In memory of HANNAH BROWN wife of Matthew Brown of Halton Red House who died July 20th 1814 aged 29 years, MATTHEW BROWN died 17th March 1867 aged 83 years

161. In memory of THOMAS JOHNSON, grocer, who died at Hexham March 11th 1862 aged 68 years, HANNAH his wife who died August 11th 1885 aged 77 years

162. Sacred to the memory of THOMAS JOHNSON of White Hall who died June 16th 1828 aged 70 years, MARY his wife died September 11th 1830 aged 74 years, THOMAS their son died November 5th 1791 aged 5 years, HANNAH their daughter died July 20th 1814 aged 29 years, SAMUEL their son died February 22nd 1826 aged 37 years, JOHN their son died at Berwick upon Tweed October 7th 1830 aged 47 years

163. In memory of MARY wife of John Armstrong, brewer, Hexham died November 12th 1854 aged 63 years

164. In loving memory of NANNY the beloved wife of John Johnson who died at Dotland Park December 4th 1904 aged 76 years, JOHN beloved husband of above who died February 27th 1906 aged 82 years

165. Here lieth the body of ELIZABETH wife of Thomas Nevin of Ardley died November 27th 1771 aged 25 years, ANN daughter of Thomas and Elizabeth died May 1773 aged 2 years

166. *A very weathered faced headstone but has angel and pair of wings engraved at top edge, vague writing on reverse, two cherubs and hour glass engraved at top edge*

167. Here lieth the body of ANN wife of Joseph Bell late of Aydonshields who departed this life January 22nd 1781 aged 63 years, JOSEPH BELL died 12th November 1786 aged 74 years

168. ELIZABETH wife of John Coulson of High Holmes died 28th February 1758 (interred at Hexham) aged 29 years, ELIZABETH daughter of John and Elizabeth Coulson died 31st January 1774 aged 15 years and 11 months, JOHN COULSON died 17th February 1774 aged 51 years
    Verse on back of stone: Spring, Summer, Autumn Reader see
    Cast fatal Darts at Us and Thee
    All our three various earthly fates
    Bear different Ages and different Dates.

Lesson instructive to thee! man
Repent in time, Life's but a span.
A winter's Death can have no sting
But what your Sins are sure to bring

169. Burial place of WILLIAM NEVIN of Park Gates died February 26th 1827 aged 82 years, GEORGE his son died May 14th 1793 aged 7 months, MARY his daughter died October 9th 1795 aged 20 years, EDWARD his son died June 13th 1815 aged 15 years, MARGARET his wife died July 15th 1822 aged 65 years. The above WILLIAM NEVIN died February 29th 1827 aged 82

170. Laid by Charlotte Fairlamb in affectionate remembrance of her brother MATTHEW EDWARD FAIRLAMB who died October 1st 1871 in the 17th year of his age and was the only son of the late John Fairlamb of Haydon Bridge

<u>Row 38</u>

171. In memory of WILLIAM BELL of Aydon Shields who died 14th August 1796 aged 80 years, WILLIAM BELL grandson of above who died 14th October 1796 aged 3 years, WILLIAM son of above died 8th April 1799

172. Sacred to the memory of ROBERT STOKOE of Chapel House who died September 6th 1832 aged 63 years, MARY his wife who died January 28th 1837 aged 63 years, also of the deceased children of John and Margaret Stokoe of Chapel House, MARY died 16th June 1868 aged 20 years, ROBERT died 10th July 1868 aged 24 years

<u>Row 39</u>

173. In remembrance of INA ALEXANDRA dearly beloved wife of Sidney L Burgess of Stotsfold Hall died 10th December 1954 and in loving memory of SIDNEY LAURENCE BURGESS died on 21st May 1970 aged 83 years

174. Here lieth the body of WILLIAM NIXON son of Thomas and Hannah Nixon of Dotland died November 29th 1767 aged 2 years and 10 months, Wm NIXON died May 30th 1771 aged 21? years and 6 months

175. In memory of JOHN RAMSAY late of Walleythorn who died at Newcastle upon Tyne 15th December 1864 aged 56, MARY ANN wife of the above and who died at Ryton October 5th 1886 aged 78 years, MARY ANN daughter of the above wife of John Smith who died at Walleythorn September 14th 1870 aged 35 years, also the above JOHN SMITH who died at Low Holmes June 20th 1893 aged 68 years, MARGARET their daughter who died at Wallsend on Good Friday 1928 aged 90 years

176. In memory of THOMAS AYDON, skinner, Hexham, who died August 1st 1825 aged 44 years, MARY his wife who died April 27th 1854 aged 75 years, JOHN son of the above died June 16th 1878 aged 68 years

177. In memory of EDWARD STEEL of Nether Mire House who died February 19th 1817 aged 96 years, ANN his wife who died September 5th 1817 aged 86 years, EDWARD son of Edward and May Steel and grandson of the above who died July 1st 1837 aged 28 years

178. In memory of ELIZABETH JOHNSON 1899 - 1985 and DOROTHY JOHNSON 1904 - 1987 of Dotland Park

179. In memory of ANNIE PICKWORTH 1901 - 1978 and ELLIS PICKWORTH 1902 - 1988 of Walley Thorn

180. In memory of THOMAS ARMSTRONG of Lilswood ob January 11th 1784/7 ?, also THOMAS his son ob June 27th 1763 aged 10 ?. ISOBELL his daughter died ob June 26th 1791..?

181. In memory of ROBERT BELL of Low Eshells who died the 4th April 1769 aged 84 years, also of JOSEPH BRIDDOCK of Fine House, Shotley, who died 7th March 1868 aged 81. ELEANOR his wife died 28th February 1870 aged 81

> *inscription on reverse: "Life how short!*
> *Eternity how long!*
> *When you read these lines you see*
> *Mind the glass that runs for thee"*
> *Memento Mori*

182. Here lies interred the body of MARY the wife of Joseph Bell of Woolley who departed this life December 1786 aged 71 years

183. In memoriam EMILIE DOROTHY ARNOLD died 26th February 1963

184. In memoriam EMILIE MARY ARNOLD died 14th March 1949

Row 40

185. In memory of JOHN CARR of Dotland Park who died 9th July 1831 aged 87, and of THOMASIN his wife who died 15th January 1793 aged 36, also of JOHN and GEORGE their sons, JOHN died 20th October 1844 aged 58, GEORGE died 20th June 1868 aged 84. They all died at Dotland Park

186. In memory of THOMASINA wife of John Carr of Dotland Park who died January 15th 1793 aged 37. MARY wife of George Davison of Marley Coat Walls died April 28th 1795 aged 67.

187. Sacred to the memory of THOMAS DIXON of Dukesfield Hall who departed this life December 6th 1823 aged 33.
inscription on back of stone:
"All you that come my grave to see
As I am so must you be
Make no delay, repent in time
For I was taken in my prime"

188. Sacred to the beloved memory of JOHN DIXON died at Hexham June 14th 1859 aged 36, also THOMAS his son died September 13th 1864 aged 7, also MARGARET his daughter died 17th February 1870 aged 16, also JOHN CARR his son died October 10th 1910 aged 54, also ELIZABETH widow of John Dixon died July 29th 1914 aged 84, also ADELE OCTAVA DIXON widow of John Carr Dixon cremated December 31st 1951 aged 88. "The Lord shall be thine everlasting light and the days of thy mourning shall be ended"

189. In memory of MARY, widow of the late Thomas Dixon agent Dukesfield Hall, who died at Juniper House June 16th 1873 aged 85. MARY youngest daughter of the above died April 15th 1841 aged 20. WILLIAM eldest son of the above died November 22nd 1841 aged 24. JANE wife of John Dixon youngest son of the above died June 20th 1853 aged 30. MARGARET only child of the above John and Jane Dixon and granddaughter of the above Mary Dixon died February 17th 1870 aged 16

33

190. *A cross with inscriptions on three sides of the base:*
East side: In memory of DORIS IRENE beloved wife of Rev. W. D. Lee died 24th March 1963 aged 50 years *South side:* Also ADA I. LEE died at York 14th May 1982. REV. W.D. (BILLY) LEE died at York 1st September 1990 *North side:* In memory of HAZEL BA. MTH. MED. dear wife of Rev. W.D.Lee died 30th May 1966 aged 54

191. Sacred to the memory of MARY the wife of Richard Ord of Dotland who died April 12th 1841 aged 60. Underneath lies the remains of an affectionate wife, a loving mother and a kind friend. She was made a Partaker of the Righteousness of Christ through Faith and is now an Inheritor of Eternal Life.

192. Here lies the body of WILLIAM TROTTER son of Michael and Mary Trotter late of the Stobb who died January 1st 1770 aged ?

193. In memory of JOHN CLOSE of Keenleywell House, Allendale who died March 23rd 1853 aged 57, and of HANNAH his wife who died October 11th 1875 aged 83. JOHN their son died October 2nd 1839 aged 8, ANN their daughter died January 2nd 1842 aged 22, THOMASIN MARGARET their daughter died July 14th 1842 aged 15, MARY their daughter died December 7th 1847 aged 25. And of RICHARD and WILLIAM THOMAS their sons who died in infancy

194. Here lieth the remains of THOMAS HARRISON of Five Dargue who died September 2nd 1786 aged 45

195. In memory of WILLIAM DINNING late of Steel who died September 9th 1825 aged 63. ANN his wife died 26th June 1838 aged 71. ANN their daughter died 18th September 1835 aged 29, WLLIAM their son died at Springwell and was buried at Usworth 29th August 1854 aged 53. Also JOHN DINNING of Lillswood who died April 15th 1879 aged 85, and of MARGERY his wife who died January 24th 1880 aged 80

196. Here lieth the body of ANN CHATT of Wagtail who died March 3rd 1773 aged 71 ?

197. Sacred to the memory of ANN TEASDALE ..? died 5th November 1833, 85 years ?

198. Sacred to the memory of ROBERT TEASDALE ..? died 22nd September 1804

199. *Base of headstone only*

200. In memory of RICHARD SMITH of Low Eshells who died May 21st 1838 aged 67, also ISABELLA his wife who died July 6th 1847 aged 88, also RICHARD their son died at High Eshells January 27th 1862 aged 69. MARY his wife died October 30th 1857 aged 65. Also of MARGARET daughter of first named Richard and Isabella who died at Low Eshells September 28th 1867 aged 65. Also of JOHN their son who died at Low Eshells September 21st 1880 aged 85. Also of THOMAS their son who died at Low Eshells April 26th 1882 aged 76

201. *Fallen stone still to be turned*

Row 41

202. ROBERT WARD of Stobbelee was buried here June 23rd 1767 aged 65. ANN daughter of Robert Ward was buried here September 29th A.D. 1767 aged 20

203. Here lies the body of JOSEPH NATTRASS of Groveyfield who departed this life April 10th 1772 aged 79

204. Here lie the bodies of JOHN NATTRASS of Lilswood who died February 10th 1797 aged 75, and of his wife MARY who died June 8th 1792 aged 70
inscription on back of stone : Hebrews 13 verse 14 "For here we have no
continuing city, but we seek one to come"
"How frail is Life! In what a narrow span
Is shut up all the transient pride of Man
Today he blooms just like the damask rose
Tomorrow pallid as the evening close
Since such is life how ....
.... the path that pointed out to thee
Thou ....love
.... thee to quit the ....
Where thou art now the ....

35

205. Here lies the body of ROBERT FOSTER of Hellewell who departed this life January 3rd A.D. 1773 aged 46
Inscription on back of stone: " Mourn not ....my decease
For I with Christ have made my peace
Life is uncertain that's most sure
Sin gave the wound Christ gave the cure"

206. In memory of WILLIAM WHALEY of Ridlemhope died November 28th 1774 aged 53

207. In loving memory of THOMAS THORBURN of Thornbrough High Barns, Corbridge who died January 3rd 1923 aged 83, also HANNAH his wife who died December 21st 1929 aged 93, also ELIZABETH their daughter who died June 16th 1955 aged 79, also ANNIE their daughter who died June 20th 1955 aged 81, also JOHN their son died March 20th 1958 aged 87, also THOMAS their son died October 12th 1958 aged 86

Row 42

208. *Inscription at top of stone: "In Christ shall all be made alive; in Adam all die"* In memory of THOMAS ADAMSON of Spitalshield who after a short illness borne with Christian resignation died December 26th 1860 aged 64. *"Let me die the death of the righteous, and let my last end be like his".* ELIZABETH his wife died April 1st 1839 aged 44. *At bottom of stone: Blessed are the dead which die in the Lord"*

209. Here lieth the body of THOMAS ADAMSON of Spittle Shield who departed this life February 6th 1782 aged 71

210. In memory of MARY wife of John Lowes of Finechambers who died the 13th March 1793 aged 30 years

211. In memory of JOHN DINNING of Tenter-House who died May 26th 1853 aged 59, also of ELIZABETH his wife who died September 11th 1880 aged 87, also JOHN their eldest son who died August 15th 1864 aged 44, also of MARGARET their youngest daughter who died July 27th 1857 aged 24. Also GEORGE DINNING who died December 28th 1901 aged 74 years. Also WILLIAM DINNING who died March 17th 1912 aged 89, also ANN SYMN wife of the above William who died January 16th 1905 aged 79

212. JOHN HESLOP deceased October 14th A.D. 1766 aged 63 years, MARY his daughter died May 26th 1773 aged 28

213. *Almost illegible - reference to records fills in space:* MARY wife of Thos Farbridge died 28th ? October 1767 aged 32. THOMAS son of Thos Farbridge died 4th January 1789

214. Here lies the body of JOHN CURRY of Stobby Lee who departed this life June 27th 1813 aged 55 years

215. In loving memory of JOSEPH beloved husband of Mary Henderson died at Rowley Head Hexhamshire September 16th 1911 aged 68. Also MARY relict of the above died at Corridge Middleton Morpeth on December 24th 1921 aged 75. Also HANNAH LIZZIE youngest daughter died January 20th 1922 aged 40

216. In memory of THOMAS WOOD of Earthly Mires who died May 15th 1810 aged 86 years, also SARAH his wife died April 1st 1814 aged 84 years

Row 43

217. The burial place of JOHN ROWLAND of Stotsfield. HANNAH daughter ob March 11th 1768 3 years 6 months, JOHN son ob July 10th 1770 11 years 6 months

218. In memory of JOHN ROWLAND of Stotsfield who died 20th February 1798 aged 78, also MARY his wife died July 27th 1822 aged 84 years. *Inscription on back of headstone:*
> *"Go home my friends and leave me here*
> *For I must lie till Christ appear*
> *A joyful rise I hope to have*
> *When Angels call me from the grave"*

219. HANNAH wife of George Armstrong of Uper Holms died November 28th 1795 aged 60 years

220. In memory of JANE widow of the late John Cox of Scotswood. She died at Low Raw Green September 3rd 1867 aged 66 years

"Unveil thy bosom, faithfull tomb,
Take this new treasure to thy trust
And give these sacred relicts room
To seek a slumber in the dust"

221. In memory of JOSEPH BLACKBURN High Staples Hexhamshire who died May 10th 1894 aged 67 years, also Catherine his wife who died at Steel Hall November 9th 1872 aged 49 years, also of JOHN second son of the above who died August 18th 1902 aged 40 years

222. *Broken tombstone, inscription is fragment only*
.... JANE ASKEW wife of Thos of Raw Green who died August 24th 1788 aged 60 ? years

Row 44

223. 34106 Private J.W. SIMPSON Northumberland Fusiliers 19th March 1917 aged 22
"Until the day breaks"

224. Here lies the body of WILLIAM NOBLE Junior who died January 4th 1787 aged 29 years. JOSEPH NOBLE departed December 15th 1786 aged 21

225. Here lies the body of CATHERINE wife of John Noble, Mollasteads who departed this life February 16th 1806 aged 67 years

Row 45

226. In loving memory of MARGARET JANE BELL daughter of John and Anne Bell of Peterel Field Hexham died December 11th 1891 aged 28, also of ROBERT her brother died February 20th 1873 aged 3 years and 11 months. Erected with funds left by the above M. J. Bell. Also the above JOHN died July 1st 1897 aged 73 and ANNE his wife died November 25th 1901 aged 74

227. BARBARA ROWLAND the wife of Robert of High Cooks House died July 26th 1777 aged 74

228. Here lies the remains of JOSEPH son of Robert and Mary Rowland who died July 2nd 1782 aged 49 years

229. In memory of GEORGE son of Thomas Carr of Dotland died May 20th 1805 aged 5 years, also HANNAH daughter of Thomas Carr died June 15th 1806 aged 2 years

230. The Burial place of THOMAS and ANNE CARR of Dotland, HANNAH their daughter died May 5th 1829 aged 21 years.
Inscription on back of headstone:
"Just like a lilly in its bloom
When in my prime I was cut down
Therefore be careful how you live
Death doth not always mourning give"

231. The burial place of HENRY ANGUS gardener, MARY his daughter died April 1803 aged 21 years. The above Henry Angus departed this life the 21st September 1810 aged 80 years
"Cheery he delved and prund; the grateful
soil with plentious crops repaid ardent toil
surprised he saw, and own'd the hand
of heaven that to his numerous household
bread was given. Around his table his lov'd
ce....s and round his house bloomed paradise anew"

232. In memory of WILLIAM ANGUS of Low Raw Green died October 19th 1859 agd 76 years, ANN his wife died at Low Raw Green July 14th 1876 aged 75 years, also ANNE ANGUS daughter of the above died at High Staples February 3rd 1900 aged 68 years, also SARAH JACKSON daughter of the above died at Low Eshells May 8th 1902 aged 76 years, also JANE FOSTER daughter of the above died May 13th 1903 aged 74 years, also MARY ANGUS daughter of the above died at Whitley Bay August 30th 1910 aged 83 years

233. In memory of WILLIAM HERON died at The Heigh November 11th 1816 aged 84 years, also his wife ELEANOR died 20th May 1789 aged 54 years, also their son JOHN died April 11th 1780 aged 1 year, also their daughter ISABELLA died 11th April 1789 aged 20 years. Also MARGARET SCOTT their sisters daughter died September 11th 1831 aged 34 years

234. In loving memory of WILLIAM SCOTT who died at The Heigh January 20th 1886 aged 85 years, also ELIZABETH his wife died April 5th 1878

aged 40 years, also ANTHONY their son died April 7th 1852 aged 10 years, also ELIZABETH their daughter died August 26th 1887 aged 48 years, also MARGARET their daughter died June 23rd 1913 aged 79 years, also WILLIAM their son died January 28th 1921 aged 75 years

235. In memory of ROBERT SCOTT The Heigh died December 7th 1858 aged 93 years, also MARY his wife died December 10th 1858 aged 87 years. The above couple was both interred in one grave. Also JOHN their son died February 3rd 1863 aged 64 years. Also DOROTHY wife of Thomas Scott son of the above parents died June 27th 1865 aged 61 years. Also the above THOMAS SCOTT died October 6th 1884 aged 78 years

Row 46

236. In memory of JOHN CARR of Dotland who died January 25th 1789 aged 57 years, also MARY his wife who died January 25th 1809 aged 77 years

237. Here lies the body of HENRY ANGUS of Blackhall who died June 26th 1775 aged 87 years

238. In memory of WILLIAM and JOHN BOWMANS sons of Joseph and Rosamond Bowmans of Jingleshaugh. William died November19th 1778 aged 21 years. John died April 6th 1779 aged 14 years.
Inscription on rear of stone: "Death like an overflowing stream
Sweeps us away our life a dream
An evening and a morning flower
Cut off and vanished in an hour"

Row 47

239. In loving memory of JOHN THOMPSON died at Earthly Mires August 14th 1892 aged 76 years, also ELIZABETH his wife died August 4th 1896 aged 84 years, also MATHEW their only son died at Whitehall June 6th 1857 aged 8 months. Also JOHN THOMPSON JAMES grandson died at Whitehall August 1st 1882 aged 7 years and 11 months, also JANE second daughter of the above and widow of the late Thomas James, Newcastle on Tyne died at Hexham April 5th 1900 aged 50 years

240. In loving memory of JOSEPH NIXON who died at Walley Thorn April 25th 1902, also ELIZABETH wife of the above who died at Walley Thorn May 2nd 1909 aged 73 years, also ROBSON son of the above who died September 12th 1931 aged 64 years, also SARAH daughter of the above who died March 7th 1935 aged 59 years

241. In loving memory of HENRY NIXON died at Walley Thorn February 20th 1930 aged 65 years

242. JOSEPH GREEN of Heckly House died November 27th 1797 aged 74 years, also LUKE GREEN of Gairshield died November 18th 1802 aged 69 years, also JOSEPH GREEN son of the above Joseph Green who died at Aydon Shields February 7th 1824 aged 59 years, also DOROTHY wife of Joseph Green senior who died at Aydon Shields April 6th 1829 aged 90 years

243. Sacred to the memory of GEORGE THIRLWELL DINNING son of William and Ann Dinning born at Steel Hexhamshire April 2nd 1809 departed this life July 25th 1900. 40 years resident in Sheffield and latterly 18 years in his native town Hexham
"For ever with the Lord through the blood of the Lamb"

244. In memory of Rev. W.J.D. WADDILOVE M.A. of Beacon Grange died October 28th 1859 aged 74 years, also ELIZABETH ANNE his wife died March 7th 1874 aged 86 years. Also in memory of JOHN ALEXANDER infant son of Admiral and Mrs. C Waddilove born December 13th 1883 died December 25th 1883. Also MARY ELIZABETH wife of Admiral Waddilove died at Admiralty House Sheerness January 10th 1888 aged 43 years. Also CHARLES L.D. WADDILOVE Admiral Royal Navy died at Beacon Grange October 17th 1896 aged 68 years. Also in memory of CHARLES JOHN DARLEY WADDILOVE eldest son of Admiral and Mrs. Waddilove killed in action in France May 4th 1917 aged 35 years

245. ISABELLA VICTORIA widow of Capt. G.E.D. Waddilove OBE born 24th May 1887 died 9th October 1972

246. Sacred to the memory of ANN TUNSTALL who died at Beacon Grange March 14th 1859 having been during the long period of 47 years the faithful

and confidential servant in the family of the Rev W.J.D. Waddilove by whom this tribute is paid in grateful remembrance of her many excellencies, unwearying services and never-failing attachment to them all

> *"Forgive blest shade the tributary tear*
> *Which mourns thy exit from a world like this*
> *Forgive the wish that would have kept thee here*
> *And stayed thy progress to the realms of bliss"*

Row 48

247. In memory of THOMAS CHARLTON of Stobby Lee who died May 10th 1872 aged 66 years, also HANNAH his wife died 6th August 1843 aged 34 years, also of ELIZABETH their daughter who died December 31st 1873 aged 40 years

248. Here lies the body of ELEIZ. daughter of Thos. Charlton of Hackford Mill died June 11th 1778 aged 18. THOS. CHARLTON died February 5th 1778 aged 77 years. THOS. son of Thos. Charlton died November 21st 1782 aged 30

Row 49

249. In loving memory of ELIZABETH AYDON of New House Hexhamshire who died March 20th 1892 aged 78 years, also WILLIAM son of the above who died December 10th 1862 aged 25 years, also MARY daughter of the above who died November 24th 1882 aged 43 years, also ROBERT CHARLTON AYDON son of the above who died March 2nd 1902 aged 57 years. Also SUSANNAH wife of Robert Charlton Aydon who died at New House July 4th 1928 aged 80 years. Also JANE MARSHALL who died September 10th 1917 aged 83 years

250. In loving memory of MARGARET EASTON wife of David Wilson of Stobby Lea who died April 5th 1915 aged 66 years, also the above DAVID who died at West Highridge Wark April 24th 1930 aged 76 years, also GEORGE EASTON third son of the above and husband of Sarah of Stotsfold Lodge who died May 29th 1964 aged 76 years late of East Uppertown Simonburn, also the above SARAH who died 16th December 1968 aged 85 years

42

251. In memory of GEORGE BARRON who died at High Staples July 9th 1863 aged 66 years, also ELIZABETH his wife who died May 10th 1858 aged 52 years, also NICHOLAS their son who died May 18th 1838 aged 5 years, also MARGARET DIXON their daughter who died at Wall December 24th 1871 aged 32 years

252. In memory of THOMAS RIDLEY of Closegreen who died July 23rd 1800 aged 78 years, also HANNAH his wife who died January 12th 1787 aged 64 years, also THOMAS their son who died March 3rd 1787 aged 21 years

253. In memory of GEORGE RIDLEY Junior of Closegreen died December 14th 1811 aged 29 years, GEORGE RIDLEY Senior Closegreen died March 4th 1814 aged 63 years, MARY RIDLEY relic of George Ridley of Closegreen died August 17th 1835 aged 90 years

inscription on back of stone: *"Farewell no more I tread your ground*
No more I need the gosple sound
My feet have reached the heavenly shore
I know no Imperfection more
For friends no more my sufferings mourn
Nor view my relicts with concern
cease to drop the pitying tear
I'm gone beyond the reach of fear

He was but room forbids to tell you what
Think what a man should be and he was that"

254. In memory of JOHN RIDLEY late of Raw Green who departed this life January 19th 1790 aged 42 years, also JOHN son of the above who died February 4th 1795 aged 9 years

"This stone was erected by William Ridley oldest son of the said John Ridley
Senior when on board His Majesty's Ship 'La Melpomene'
Oh cruel death that would not spare
My loving Sire, my Brother dear
Both they are gone, left me behind
The world to try and friends to find"

255. *A square stone with inscriptions on three sides - South:* Sacred to the memory of THOMAS RIDLEY son of John Ridley of Row Green died at Juniper April 24th 1836 aged 61 years and was buried here,

also MARGARET DINNING his wife who died at Juniper February 5th 1844 aged 73 years and was buried here *East* JOHN RIDLEY of Hexham Civil Engineer son of Thomas Ridley and Margaret Dinning died at Redcar January 19th 1876 aged 81 years and was buried here, also ISABELLA DAWSON his first wife died at Acklington June 22nd 1826 aged 24 years and was buried at Warkworth, also ANN MATTESON his second wife who died at Hexham December 27th 1875 aged 83 years and was buried here *North:* Thomas Dawson Ridley son of John Ridley and Isabella Dawson, Civil Engineer erected this monument near which lie the remains of four generations of his ancestors. In memory of the above mentioned THOMAS DAWSON RIDLEY born at Acklington on February 4th 1825 died at Coatham, Redcar January 13th 1898 buried at Redcar

256. Erected in affection and in remembrance of WILLIAM son of William and Sarah Taylor of Juniper died July 13th 1874 aged 25 years and GEORGE their son died May 10th 1876 aged 31 years, and also of the above WILLIAM TAYLOR died April 22nd 1878 aged 61 years, also SARAH wife of above William Taylor died August 7th 1899 aged 87 years, also JOSHUA SMITH nephew of above died September 26th 1927 aged 89 years

Row 50

257. In memory of ANNIE wife of Isaac Herdman who died at The Vance, Langley February 13th 1830 aged 73 years

258. In loving memory of WILLIAM HERDMAN who died at Cockplay, Humshaugh December 12th 1881 aged 66 years interred at Beltingham, also JANE his wife who died at Raw Green April 10th 1895 aged 72 years, also SEPTIMUS their son who died August 23rd 1877 aged 18 years interred at Beltingham, also EDWARD their son who died at Raw Green April 26th 1900 aged 48 years, also WILLIAM their son who died at Raw Green December 27th 1925 aged 77 years

259. In loving memory of BARBARA the beloved wife of George Bell of Stotsfold who died April 4th 1910 aged 62 years, also GEORGE BELL died March 30th 1924 aged 77 years, also EDWARD JOSEPH BELL grandson of above died January 10th 1932 aged 21 years the son of George Edward and Ada Bell, and also of the above GEORGE EDWARD died February

11th 1950 aged 76 years, also ADA his wife died January 9th 1955 aged 81 years

<u>Row 51</u>

260. In memory of WILLIAM RODDAM who died at Litterage Lodge December 10th 1879 aged 64 years, also MARGERY his wife who died at Haltwhistle April 19th 1898 aged 85 years, also ROBERT RODHAM son of above of Red Lead Mill who died September 5th 1903 aged 55 years, also MARGARET RODDAM who died at Low Raw Green March 30th 1886 aged 35 years

261. In memory of GEORGE GOLIGHTLY died 1825 aged 62 , also JANE his wife died 1829 aged 69, also their sons and daughters GEORGE died 1798 aged 13 ANTHONY died 1806 aged 18, JAMES died 1824 aged 40, HARMON died 1838 aged 46, SARAH died 1841 aged 47, JANE died 1879 aged 79

CHAPTER 2

OLD CHURCHYARD INDEX OF SURNAMES
(numbers refer to headstone plan)

ADAMSON Thomas, Elizabeth 208; Thomas 209.

ALLCROFT Hannah, William 37.

ANDERSON Thomas, Hannah, Richard, John, Mary 13; Dorothy Ann, John Robson, John George, William, Dorothy, Lancelot 95.

ANGUS William, Isabella 127; Henry, Mary 231; William, Anne, Ann, Sarah, Mary 232; Henry 237.

ARMSTRONG Thomas William, Grace, Cpl. Fred 86; John, Barbara Jane 90; William, Elizabeth 151; Robert I. 103; Mary 163; Thomas, Isobell 180; Hannah 219.

ARNOLD Emilie Dorothy 183; Emilie Mary 184.

ARTLEY Barbara, Thomas 140.

ASKEW Jane 222.

ATKINSON Ann 88; Lillian, John 94.

AYDON Thomas, Mary, John 176; Elizabeth, William, Mary, Robert Charlton, Susannah 249.

BALDERSON Robert Anderson 84.

BARRON George, Elizabeth, Nicholas 251.

BATEY Nicholas Sparke, Isabell 97.

BELL John, Elizabeth 48; Michael, Annie, Rebecca 76; Robert, Mary Ann, Elizabeth 102; Ann 132; William, Elizabeth, John, Catherine, Sarah Jane 142; Elizabeth, John, Ann, Hannah 143; Ann, Joseph 167; William, William Bell 171; Robert 181; Mary 182; Margaret Jane, Robert, John, Anne 226; Barbara, George, Edward Joseph, George Edward, Ada 259.

BIRKS Robert Charlton, Elizabeth 109.

BLACKBURN Joseph, Catherine, John 221.

BOLAM John, Jane 59.

BOWMANS William, John 238.

BRIDDOCK Joseph, Eleanor 181.

BRISCOE Thomas 131.

BROWN The Rev. Abraham, Alice 101; Hannah, Matthew 160.

BURGESS Sidney Laurence, Ina Alexandra 173.

CAMPBELL William Gordon 71.

CARR Samuel, Sarah, Florence Ellenor, John Henry 63; John, Thomasin,

George 185; Thomasina, Mary 186; George, Hannah 229; Thomas, Anne, Hannah 230; John, Mary 236.

CHARLTON John 11; Anthony Elliot, Anthony Forster 53; George 85; Robert Blackett, Mary Ellen 96; Robert, Mary, Elizabeth, Ann 110; Thomas, Hannah, Elizabeth 247; Eleiz, Thomas 248.

CHATT Joseph, Jane 25; Ann 196.

CLARK Matthew Henry, Meggie 77; Mary Ann, William, Thomas William 78.

CLOSE John, Hannah, Ann, Thomasin Margaret, Mary, Richard, William 193.

COMMON Annie Ellen, Mary Ann, James 68.

CONNELL Florence Ada 96.

COOK Anthony, George Carr, Emily, Cicely, William, Jane, Margery 43; Margaret Jane, Thomas Dixon, Jane 44.

CORBY Mollie 111.

COULSON Elizabeth, John 168.

COWING Matthew, Mary Ann, Abram, Isabell, Frances, George Anthony, Mildred 35.

COX Jane 220.

CROSS Laura 56; Jack Brian 57.

CUMMINGS George 53.

CURREY William, Ann Bell, Margaret, Robert, Mildred 132.

CURRY John, Mildred, Matthew, Thomas 106; John 214.

DAGG Agnes121.

DAVIDSON George, Rebecca 2; Jane 3.

DAWSON Isabella 255.

DINNING John, Margaret, James, Ann Jane, Margery, Thomasin Ann 61; William, Ann, John, Margery 195; John, Elizabeth, Margaret, George, William, Ann 211; George Thirlwell 243; Margaret 255.

DIXON Margaret, Joseph 72; George Anthony 99; Elizabeth, Margaret, Thomas, Mary 128; William, Hannah, John 129; Robert, Ann, Hannah 144; Hannah, Edward 145; Henry, Margaret 146; Joseph, Mary, Isabella, Peter, Ann 147; Edward, Margaret 150; Percival, Bell 154; Thomas 187; John, Thomas, Margaret, Elizabeth, Adele Octava 188; Mary, William, Jane Margaret 189; Margaret 251.

DODD William, Sarah, Joseph, Thomas, Isaac, Ruth 32; William, Anne, Mary, Thomas, James, Frances, Evelyn Mary 38; James, Mildred 132; Michael, Mary, Margaret, Eleanor, William, Thomasin 133; Thomas, Mary, John, George Charlton, Frances 134; John Thomas 135.

EASTON Margaret, David, George, Sarah 250.

ERRINGTON Robert 36; John 39; Robert 40; Mary, Thomas 41; Thomas Foster, Hannah 42.

FAIRLAMB Jane 136; Matthew Edward 170.

FAIRLESS Joseph, Mary 67.

FEATHERSTON Barbara, John, Margaret, Wharton, Thomas 112.

FORREST Douglas? 104; William Anderson, John Christopher 105.

FORSTER John, Margaret, Catherine 9; Mary 26; Hannah 102.

FOSTER Robert 205; Jane 232.

GOLIGHTLY George, Jane, Anthony, James Harmon, Sarah 261.

GREEN Joseph, Luke, Dorothy 242.

HALL Thomas, Susannah, Elizabeth, Thomas 33; Margaret 81.

HARBOTTLE Mary Ann 47.

HARDING Annie Alice 108; Edward, Margaret 116.

HARKNESS David John 87.

HARRISON Hannah 15; Thomas 194.

HEDLEY Ephraim, Eleanor, Elizabeth Catherine, Joseph, John 60.

HENDERSON Joseph, Hannah Lizzie 215.

HERDMAN Annie 257; William, Jane, Septimus, Edward 258.

HERON William 108; William, Eleanor, John, Isabella 233.

HOGARTH William, Ann, Robert, Margaret 125.

HOOK Thomas 21.

JEWITT Prudhoe 8.

JOHNSON Anthony, Ann, George 126; William 155; Mary Hannah, John 156; John, Mary, William 158; John 159; Thomas, Hannah 161; Thomas, Mary, Hannah, Samuel, John 162; Elizabeth, Dorothy 178.

KENNEDY Sarah Hannah 119; Henry 120; Agnes, William 121; Margaret Annie 122; Betty 123.

KIRSOPP Elizabeth 54.

LAIDLER Margaret 5.

LAING Ann, Andrew 52.

LAMB Jane, Dorothy, John 24.

LEATHARD Elizabeth 138.

LEE Doris Irene, Ada I., Rev. William, Hazel 190.

LEYBOURNE John Angus 69.

LINSLEY George 152.

LISHMAN Joseph 80.

LITTLE Edie, Robert, Adam Robert 1; Helen, George Davidson, Agnes, Mary Jane, David, Helen, Robert 3; Gordon 22; Thomas William 81.

LOWES Mary 210.

MARSHALL Ellen 53; Jane 249.

MATTESON Ann 255.

MAUGHAN Margaret H, William 62.

MOORE Thomas, Jane Ann 83.

MORALEE Fred J., Ada 58.

NATTRASS Joseph 203; John, Mary 204.

NATTRESS Mary Emma, Hannah, Eliza 31

NEILSON James, Hannah, Alexander, Mary Jane, Ann Ellen 70.

NEVIN Joseph William, Joseph, Isaac 89; Elizabeth, Ann 165; William, George, Edward, Margaret 169.

NICHOL Thomas, Hannah, Samuel, Sarah, Mary Elizabeth, Mary 64.

NIXON William 174; Joseph, Elizabeth, Robson, Sarah 240; Henry 241.

NOBLE William, Joseph 224; Catherine 225.

OLIVER George, Mary, John Bell 45; Ann 143; William, Hannah Helen 153.

ORD Mary 191.

PATRICK Alexander, Annie 59; Ralph, Thomasina Margaret 74.

PAUL William, Dorothy 47.

PICKERING Jane, Ralph 27; Sarah, William, Joseph 51.

PICKWORTH Angus 157; Annie, Ellis 179.

PIGG Jane, Edward, Thomas, Joseph 5.

RAMSAY John, Mary Ann, John Smith, Margaret 175.

REAY John, Catherine 79.

REED George William 10; Mary Ann 89; William, Robert 141.

RICHARDSON John, Dorothy 130.

RIDLEY Thomas, Hannah 252; George, Mary 253; John 254; Thomas, Margaret, John, Thomas Dawson, Isabella, Ann 255.

ROBSON George, Mary Ellen 12; Mary Hannah, Thomas 46; Mary, John, Isabella; Mary Jane 50; John, George William 107, Henry, Frances Jane, Frances Evelyn 108.

RODDAM Margery 55; William, Margery, Robert, Margaret 260.

ROSS Joan 65.

ROWLAND John, Hannah 217; John, Mary 218; Barbara 227; Joseph 228.

SCOTT Richard 17; Jane 18; James 19; Archibald 20; Margaret 233; William, Elizabeth, Anthony, Margaret 234; Robert, Mary, John, Dorothy, Thomas 235.

SIMPSON Thomas, John White, Annie Ursula, Ann, Christopher, Jane 148; J.W. 223.

SISSON Rev. William 117; Elizabeth 118.

SISTERSON William, John, Elizabeth, Matthew 6.

SMITH Clarence Dalrymple, Cicely 115; Richard, Isabella, Mary, Margaret, John, Thomas 200; Joshua 256.

SOPPITT Hannah 144.

STEEL Joshua, Edward, Frances 136; Edward 177.

STOBBS Nicholas, Margery 23; Edward Dalton, Catherine 82.

STOKOE William, Ann 73; Robert, Mary 172.

STOWELL Robert Cowen 84.

SYMN Mary, William, Cuthbert, John 34; Ann 211.

TAYLOR Isabella 16; William, George, Sarah 256.

TEASDALE Ann 197; Robert 198.

TELFER John, Margaret Ann, Lizzie 124.

THOMPSON Elizabeth, John, Mathew John James, Jane 239.

THORBURN Andrew 29; Richard, Margaret, John William 30; James, Mary, Andrew 37.

THORNBURN John, James, Francis, Richard, Ann 28; Thomas, Hannah, Elizabeth, Annie, John 207.

TINLIN Anne 149.

TROTTER William 192.

TUNSTALL Ann 246.

TURNBULL Edward H. 7; Robert James, Hannah, John 75.

TWEDDLE Richard, John, Alice Jane, Hannah Francis 66.

URWIN Thomas, Isabella Margaret 98.

WADDILOVE Rev. W.J.D., Elizabeth Anne, John Alexander, Mary Elizabeth, Charles L.D., Charles John Darley 244; Isabella Victoria 245.

WALTON William, Jane 15.

WANLACE Joseph, Sarah, Jane, John, Lancelot 139.

WARD Robert, Ann 202.

WATSON Sarah, George, William 91; George, Pearson Pringle, John, George Bell, Arthur 100.

WHALEY William 206.

WHITE John, Ann 4; Matthew, Mary 14; Thomas, Annie 92; Matthew Henry, Thomas Sidney, William, John William, Jane, Arthur Leonard 93; George, Mary 137.

WOOD Thomas, Sarah 216.

YARROW Jane 100.

UNMARKED BURIALS IN THE OLD CHURCHYARD

NAME	AGE	DATE OF BURIAL	DWELLING
ANDERSON Anthony	4 weeks	13.3.1853	Lillswood
ANDERSON Edward	29	1.9.1850	Shiel Hall
ANDERSON Hannah	79	8.5.1854	Dipton Mill
ANDERSON John	21	29.1.1855	Traveller's Rest Cottage
ANDERSON William	81	25.8.1858	Traveller's Rest Cottage
ARCHER Sarah	1 day	23.4.1851	The Lee
ARMSTRONG Hannah		4.10.1767	Stobbilee
ARMSTRONG Isabell		19.8.1778	
ARMSTRONG Sarah		28.9.1767	Stobbilee
ARMSTRONG Thomas		18.4.1776	Dotland Fell
ARMSTRONG William	81	25.8.1858	Riddlehamhope
ARTLEY Mary		1.4.1772	Newbiggin
ASKEW Joseph	65	30.5.1854	Raw Green Shop
ATKINSON Joseph	45	7.11.1859	Doddery Shield
BELL Ann	46	12.12.1857	Barker House
BELL Elizabeth		19.7.1775	High Raw Green
BELL Elizabeth		6.10.1776	Low Eshalls
BELL Frances	65	24.1.1858	Blackhall Mill
BELL George		4.11.1770	High Raw Green
BELL James	35	19.8.1854	Hallington
BELL Jane	79	29.5.1856	Dalton
BELL John	2 days	12.5.1861	Mollersteads
BELL John	73	1.7.1897	
BELL John		17.5.1774	High Raw Green
BELL Mary	91	7.6.1860	Middle Dukesfield
BELL Mary	79	14.2.1858	The Lee
BELL Mary		22.12.1766	Peacock House
BELL Matthew		28.9.1765	Embley
BELL Robert	9 hours	12.5.1861	Mollersteads

BELL Robert	72	10.5.1860	Hesleywell
BELL Robert		30.5.1768	Aydon Sheals
BELL Thomas		23.10.1765	Bush
BLACKBURN Jonathon		25.5.1696	
BOWMAN Anne		7.4.1771	Steele
BOWMAN Joseph		14.8.1774	Steele
BOWMAN Margaret	80	15.12.1854	Fine Chambers
BOWMAN Margaret		11.4.1770	Steele
BOWMAN Mary		28.12.1770	Hathery Burn
BOWMAN Mary		16.4.1771	Steele
BOWMAN Thomas		25.1.1770	Heathery Burn
BRIDDICK Ann	68	30.5.1853	High Lillswood
BRIDDICK Matthew	70	16.5.1852	High Lillswood
BRONLEY William D.	1	21.9.1860	The Holmes
BROWN John	52	22.1.1854	Lightside
BROWN Sarah (infant)		13.3.1699	
BULMAN Isaac		5.9.1770	Upper Eshalls
BULMAN Margaret		18.2.1765	High Dalton
BULMAN Sarah	50	4.3.1858	Dye House
BULMAN Thomas		4.6.1770	High Dalton
CANT Elizabeth		30.8.1775	Steele
CARR George		9.8.1769	Dotland Park
CARR George		22.1.1776	Peacockhouse
CARR Henry	90	16.2.1855	High Park House
CARR Joseph	7 months	3.5.1855	Channel Well
CARR Joseph		26.12.1770	Dotland
CARR Thomas		6.12.1773	Finechambers
CARRICK John		14.5.1766	Red Lead Mill
CHARLTON Ann	75	2.8.1852	Dye House
CHARLTON Hannah	2	24.10.1860	Dye House
CHARLTON Joseph	87	2.8.1856	Stobby Lee
CHARLTON Margaret	64	3.11.1859	Hexham
CHARLTON Thomas	75	17.6.1850	Green-ways
CHATT Jane		12.12.1766	Low Dalton
CHATT Mary	46	13.8.1856	Red House
CLEMISON Anne		19.10.1765	Chapelhouse
CLEMISON John		23.9.1768	High Dalton
CLEMISON Nicholas		11.5.1772	High Dalton
CLEMISON Robert		5.3.1771	High Dalton

COWEN William	69	26.9.1858	Embley
CURREY Esther	45	31.8.1856	Winter House
CURREY Hunter ?	46	6.11.1851	Hole House
CURREY John	73	18.7.1855	Blackhall Mill
CURREY John		3.1.1774	Hexham Fell
CURRY John	55	27.6.1813	StobbyLee
DAVISON Mary	67	25.4.1795	
DAVISON Michael	22	31.8.1851	Loadman
DAVISON William	11	3.6.1858	High Lilswood
DENT Jane		25.10.1776	Allendale
DINNING Thomasin	8	20.2.1851	Lillswood
DIXON Anne		13.3.1776	Mollersteads
DIXON Catherine		6.5.1766	Mollersteads
DIXON Edward		21.6.1772	Mollersteads
DIXON Elizabeth	2 days	17.1.1861	High Staples
DIXON Elizabeth	82	12.7.1857	Spital Shield
DIXON Elizabeth		30.11.1764	Mollersteads
DIXON George	72	22.6.1850	Spittal Shield
DIXON Hannah	29	7.10.1765	Mollersteads
DIXON Henry		1.5.1770	Upper Stapples
DIXON Joseph	75	28.2.1857	Juniper
DIXON Joseph		13.12.1769	Woodside
DIXON Margaret	42	28.3.1859	The Steel
DIXON Mary	72	25.2.1859	Juniper
DIXON Robert	3	12.6.1851	Lee Moor House
DIXON Robert	80	15.12.1851	Woodley Field Cottage
DIXON William		8.6.1770	Chapel House
DUNN Jane Ann	1	28.2.1855	The Hill
DUNN Mary Jane	2 days	10.2.1852	Newbiggin Hill
ELLERINGTON John	81	6.8.1850	The High Juniper
ELLERINGTON Mary	22	29.6.1859	Hexham
ELLERINGTON Thomas	18	22.8.1860	Hexham
ELLERY George	75	11.12.1859	High Side
ELLIOT Hannah	9 months	7.6.1856	Brunt Rig
ELLIOTT William	66	18.10.1860	The Nether Holmes
ERRINGTON Ann		16.11.1765	Whitehall
ERRINGTON Hannah	76	3.8.1854	Whitley Cottage
ERRINGTON Joseph	4	3.8.1852	Dalton

ERRINGTON Mary	46	2.2.1850	Hamburn hall
ERRINGTON Thomas	53	16.6.1852	Hamburn Hall
FAIRLAMB Richard	52	9.3.1852	The Lee
FARBRIDGE Sarah	38	25.5.1850	The Lee
FARBRIDGE Thomas	57	25.7.1850	The High Stapples
FARROW Joseph	30	25.6.1855	Black Hill
FORREST Mary		20.1.1766	Parkhouse
FORSTER Hannah	47	22.2.1859	Parkhouse
FORSTER Hannah	80	13.4.1856	
FORSTER Jane	85	13.2.1855	Pasture House
FORSTER John	17	9.3.1849	Winnis-Hill
FORSTER John	91	23.4.1855	Low House
FORSTER Margaret		13.6.1775	High Dalton
FORSTER Mary	62	24.4.1853	Red Lead Mill
FORSTER Mary	3	16.12.1855	Whitley Chapel School
FORSTER William	13 days	3.1.1858	Dye House
FOSTER John		19.6.1775	Lee
GALLON Margaret		4.12.1775	Cooke's House
GILLIS Matthew	70	13.9.1850	Slaley
GILLIS William	33	27.2.1849	New House
GLENWRIGHT Hannah		11.9.1773	Upper Stapples
GLENWRIGHT Hugh		25.8.1769	Whitley Mill hill
GLENWRIGHT Mary		13.7.1773	Whitley Mill hill
GRAHAM Ann		26.3.1767	Fogget
GRAHAM Barbara	21	28.8.1854	Woodside
GRAHAM Elizabeth	25	8.4.1854	Woodside
GRAHAM Robert	66	18.12.1852	Woodside
GREEN George		14.10.1765	Mollersteads
GREEN George		30.5.1773	Turfhouse
GREEN Mary		27.2.1765	Turfhouse
GREEN Sarah		2.3.1776	Turfhouse
GREEN William	13	20.11.1856	High Juniper
GREEN William	64	12.12.1857	Lee Moor House
HALL George		1.4.1768	Heigh
HALL Jane		2.3.1773	St. John Lee
HALL John		16.12.1767	Heigh
HALL Joseph	20	11.2.1857	Pasture House
HALL Margaret		7.10.1941	
HALL William	15	19.3.1858	Pasture House

HARDY Jacob	19	7.3.1861	Edes Bush
HARLE Alice		22.3.1775	Ordley
HARRISON Anne		1.6.1770	Five Dargue
HARRISON Mary		16.10.1776	Loaning House
HENDERSON Edward	6 days	1.12.1854	Ordley
HENDERSON Elizabeth	48	13.5.1852	Meeting House (Finechambers?)
HENDERSON John		23.6.1775	Stotsfold
HENDERSON Mary		5.9.1766	Mirehouse
HENDERSON Robert		11.5.1771	Mire Houses
HENDERSON Sarah	40	26.11.1854	Ordley
HERON William	75	10.4.1851	The Heigh
HESLOP Mary	28	26.5.1773	Cockershields
HESLOP Mary Ann	4	15.11.1858	Stotsfold
HILL Margaret		26.11.1766	Embley Groove
HIND/MAUGHAN Martha		6.4.1768	Hexham
HODGSON John		24.3.1700	'a poor travellingman who died at Peacock House'
HODGSON Utrick	60	26.1.1854	Shellah Green
HOLDEN George	1 day	9.12.1850	Juniper
HOWDEN/BURNET Mary		3.5.1771	Ovingham
HUDSPITH James	40	19.10.1848	
HUTCHINSON Elizabeth	1	30.12.1852	Peth Foot
HUTCHINSON Isabella	3	27.12.1852	Peth Foot
HUTCHINSON Michael	87	16.8.1854	Gallas Quarry
JOBLING Susanna		23.2.1769	Stone Houses
JOHNSON Joseph	68	1.8.1849	Whitley Cottage
JOHNSON Mary	79	14.4.1853	Slaley
JOHNSON Mary		19.7.1772	Hathery Burn
JOHNSON Mary		10.4.1774	Whitehall
JOHNSON Robert		25.12.1772	Dotland Fell
JOHNSON Thomas	66	1.3.1857	Hexham
JOHNSON Thomas		22.3.1777	Whitehall
JOHNSON William		23.6.1776	Whitehall
LAMB Jane	9 months	27.2.1860	Lee Grange
LEATHARD Mary	74	22.5.1851	Hexham
LEE George	71	2.4.1857	The Holmes
LITTLE Agnes	1 month	19.8.1855	Harwood Shield

LITTLE George	8	26.6.1855	Harwood Shield
MAUGHAN Elizabeth		14.8.1773	Mollersteads
MAUGHAN Elizabeth	25	8.8.1858	Dukesfield Hall
MAUGHAN John		19.9.1764	Mollersteads
MAUGHAN Sarah		9.4.1769	Mollersteads
MAUGHAN William		19.9.1774	Mollersteads
MIDDLETON Edward		8.12.1773	Fenhouse
MIDDLETON Joseph		27.1.1704	Fenhouse
NATTRASS Matthew		20.8.1773	Growseyfield, alias Steel
NATTRASS Thomas		26.7.1776	Black Hall
NEVIN Christopher	78	28.4.1854	Dipton House, Corbridge
NEWBEGIN Mary	6	21.4.1861	Finechambers Mill
NEWBIGGIN Thomas	10	10.9.1860	Finechambers Mill
NICHOLSON Elizabeth	81	23.1.1856	Dalton
NICHOLSON George		11.2.1773	Dotland Fell
NICHOLSON John	81	3.7.1853	Intack
NIXON Frances	75	27.12.1858	Barker house
NIXON Mary	3	28.12.1859	Ivy Cottage
NIXON Mary	37	9.7.1854	Smelting Syke
NIXON Mary	14 days	9.7.1854	Smelting Syke
NIXON Robson	5 days	13.5.1852	Smelting Syke
NIXON Thomas	33	27.11.1860	The Lee
NOBLE Ann		27.5.1765	Lillswood
OLIVER Margaret		25.5.1775	Ordley
OLIVER Thomas	11 mnths	25.11.1860	Dotland
ORD Cuthbert		14.1.1767	Harwood Shield
ORD Matthew	33	20.5.1854	The Steel
ORD William		13.1.1769	High Dalton
PRATT Ann	48	22.6.1852	Hexham
PRATT Frances Jane	3	14.5.1856	Hexham
PURVIS Ann	3	11.4.1852	The Steel
PURVIS Barbara		17.3.1767	Steele
PURVIS Barbara		8.5.1776	Steele
PURVIS Joseph	15	28.9.1852	The Steel
PURVIS Thomas		13.10.1771	Steele
PURVIS Thomas		8.10.1775	Steele
RAIN William		11.7.1767	Low Dalton
RAINE Ann		23.7.1776	Heigh
RAY Thomas		5.9.1767	Redlead Mill

REED Robert	16	3.10.1772	Dotland
REED/COWIN Martha		4.9.1765	Coastley Mill
RIDLEY Anne		2.2.1770	Dipton Mill
RIDLEY Isabella	4	1.5.1852	Woolley
RIDLEY Jane	43	19.7.1852	Woolley
RIDLEY John	1	4.9.1859	Dye House
RIDLEY Ralph		25.3.1772	Dipton Mill
RIDLEY Sarah	27	2.1.1859	Woolley
RIDLEY Sarah	75	22.5.1854	Woolley
RITSON Elizabeth		24.12.1775	Winterhouse
ROBINSON Jane	45	11.11.1855	Peacock House
ROBSON John	13 days	16.2.1860	Gairshield
ROBSON Mary	54	5.5.1855	Gairshield
ROBSON Mary	43	11.10.1855	Lowe's Fell
ROBSON Mary Ann	17	25.3.1859	Todridge
ROBSON Thomas		24.5.1772	Lee
ROSS John		16.6.1775	North Britain
ROUTLEDGE Edward	74	10.1.1858	Walley Thorn
ROWLAND Robert	84	24.5.1852	Barker House
RUDWICK Margaret		28.12.1768	Hexham
SCOTT Elizabeth	48	5.3.1858	Hexham
SCOTT Mary	37	30.8.1857	Miremeadows
SCOTT Mary Ann	11	26.11.1850	Black Hall Mill
SHAW Elizabeth	4	7.6.1858	White Hall
SHAW Mary Jane	11months	29.6.1858	White Hall
SHAW Matthew Robson	1	10.6.1852	Edes Bush
SHIPLEY William		20.3.1776	Whitehall
SIMM Hannah	25	21.1.1860	Peth Foot
SIMM John	3	20.11.1856	Peth Foot
SIMPSON John		11.1.1773	Hesley Well
SIMPSON Mary		5.5.1775	Blackhall Mill
SMITH Thomasin	60	17.3.1857	Spital Shield
STAWPERT Hannah		17.4.1775	Stobbhall
STAWPERT Margaret		23.9.1768	Steele
STAWPERT Margaret		23.12.1770	Barkerhouse
STEELE Anne		12.5.1773	Low Ardley
STEELE Edward		25.3.1770	Litteredge
STEELE John		31.10.1774	Dukesfield Hall
STEELE Joshua	16	15.1.1772	Wooley Mill

STEELE Margaret		8.4.1771	Steele
STEELE Margaret		3.1.1765	Upper Staples
STOBBS Elizabeth		12.7.1767	Mire Meadows
STOBBS Hannah		6.6.1773	Westermeadows
STOBBS Margaret	40	5.7.1858	Heathery Haugh
STOBBS Margaret	40	20.10.1857	Peth Head
STOBBS Mary	17months	14.4.1856	Turf House
STOBBS Matthew	60	11.4.1857	Lillswood
STOBBS Nicholas		26.3.1775	Hathery Haugh
STOBBS Robert	2 days	4.4.1854	Heathery Haugh
STOBBS Thomas	9	5.1.1861	Fine Chambers
STOBBS William		4.12.1771	Upper Eshalls
STOKER Jane		6.2.1774	Turfhouse
STOKOE John	3	24.3.1861	Ordley
TAYLOR Hannah	64	18.4.1849	The Smelting Syke
TAYLOR Robert	67	16.1.1856	Low Smelting Syke
TAYLOR William		26.4.1766	Smelting Syke
TEASDALE Elizabeth	57	2.3.1854	Hexham
TEASDALE Mary	77	5.4.1856	Allendale
THIRLWALL Frances		20.11.1769	Closes Yates
THIRLWALL Mary		7.10.1771	Mollersteads
THIRLWALL Peter		22.3.1772	Closes Yates
THIRLWALL Thomas		16.4.1772	Closes Yates
THOMPSON Robert	50	7.8.1850	Butchers Bank
TROTTER Michael		24.10.1775	Blackhall
WALTON Joseph		7.7.1771	Lee
WALTON William		26.9.1765	Chapelhouse
WARD Anne	20	30.9.1767	Stobbilee
WARD George	94	18.5.1851	Gingleshaugh
WARDELL Jane	71	1.8.1855	Barker House
WARDLE Thomas	77	26.8.1857	Barker House
WATSON Ann Jane	5	17.8.1858	The Letch
WEAR Eliz. d.o. of 'Duke		23.7.1713	Stapples
WHITE George		3.10.1775	Steele
WHITE Mary		2.1.1777	Steele
WIGHAM William	86	27.12.1850	Dotland
WILKINSON Margaret	20	19.4.1849	Dotland
WILSON Elizabeth		28.3.1774	Turfhouse
WINTER John	37	13.12.1859	Mire House

WINTER Mary	26	13.8.1854	Mire House
WINTER Mary		14.4.1772	Dotland
WINTER Michael	23	18.4.1855	White Hall
WOOD William		8.9.1765	Dotland
WOODNESS John		20.4.1765	Lillswood

NO GRAVEN STONE

No graven stone
Marked her last bed ;
But at her head
A lilac-tree.
Where all alone
She'd made her bed
A lilac shed
Its fragrancy
Above her head.
No stone, she said
No stone for me :
When I alone
Lie quietly
Set at my head
No lifeless stone ;
But plant instead
A living tree.

Wilfrid Wilson Gibson
(1878 - 1964)

THE NAMELESS HEADSTONE

Above the time-obliterated mound
Still stands the headstone : but the graven name
Has all shaled off ; and no man may recall
Who is the tenant of this little plot.

Yet when he died the world came to an end –
The world whose centre was his consciousness,
A world of hills and rivers, fields and woods,
Sunlit and starry skies, a world of men,
Of loves and hates and dreams and ecstasies,
An individual world that only in
His heart existed – his heart that in its compass
Held a whole universe by God created
For him and him alone, by God who died
Within him as the light failed, and as all
The imagination of his heart was darkened .   .   .

Yet of the man and of the universe
That perished with his passing no memorial
Remains, save this blank shaling slab of stone.

Wilfrid Wilson Gibson
(1878 - 1964)

CHAPTER 4

MEMORIALS INSIDE CHURCH
Numbered anticlockwise from right of church door

1. *Window* - In thanksgiving to God for MURIEL TWEDDLE of the Lea Farm 1920 - 1990

2. *Inset marble plaque* - In memory of ANN PRATT of Hexham who died on the 19th June 1852 aged 48 years. Also of FRANCES JANE daughter of the above who died on the 12th May 1856, aged 3 years and 11 months.

3. *Stained glass window* - To the Glory of God and in memory of WILLIAM ANGUS. This window is dedicated by his widow Isabella Angus.

4. *Inset marble plaque* - To the Glory of God and in memory of THE REV. ARTHUR LEES, vicar of this parish 1906 - 1917. Erected by his parishioners.

5. *Oak panelling either side of alter* - To the Glory of God and in memory of THE REVEREND WILLIAM SISSON, vicar of this parish 1841 - 1906.

6. *Brass plaque below large stained glass window behind alter* - To the Glory of God, Given with £400 in trust for the poor, in memory of SAMUEL and THOMASINA JOHNSON, natives of this Chapelry, by their son THOMAS, who died at Spa House, Scremerston January 18th 1894 aged 74 years.

7. *Small brass plaque* - This aumbry and lamp were given in memory of JACK BRIAN CROSS of Dotland Grange 1916 - 1981.

8. *Inset marble plaque* - Sacred to the memory of JOHN JOHNSON of Hamburn Hall who died 20th April 1834 aged 83 years and of MARY his wife who died 20th April 1810 aged 56 years.

9. *Stained glass window* - To the Glory of God and in loving memory of JOHN JOHNSON of Dotland Park who died Feb 27th 1906, and of NANNY his wife who died Dec 4th 1904.

10. *Engraving on oak lectern* - To the Glory of God and in loving memory of BARBARA ERRINGTON.

11. *Window* - In thanksgiving to God for JOHN ANDREW REED of High Eshells 1970 - 1990.

12. *Stained glass window* - This window celebrates 2000 years of Christian worship through images associated with St. Cuthbert. It was crafted by Bridget Jones from original drawings by local children.

13. *Noticeboard framed with light oak* - In memory of JOHN CARTER 1932 - 1995.

Lower churchyard

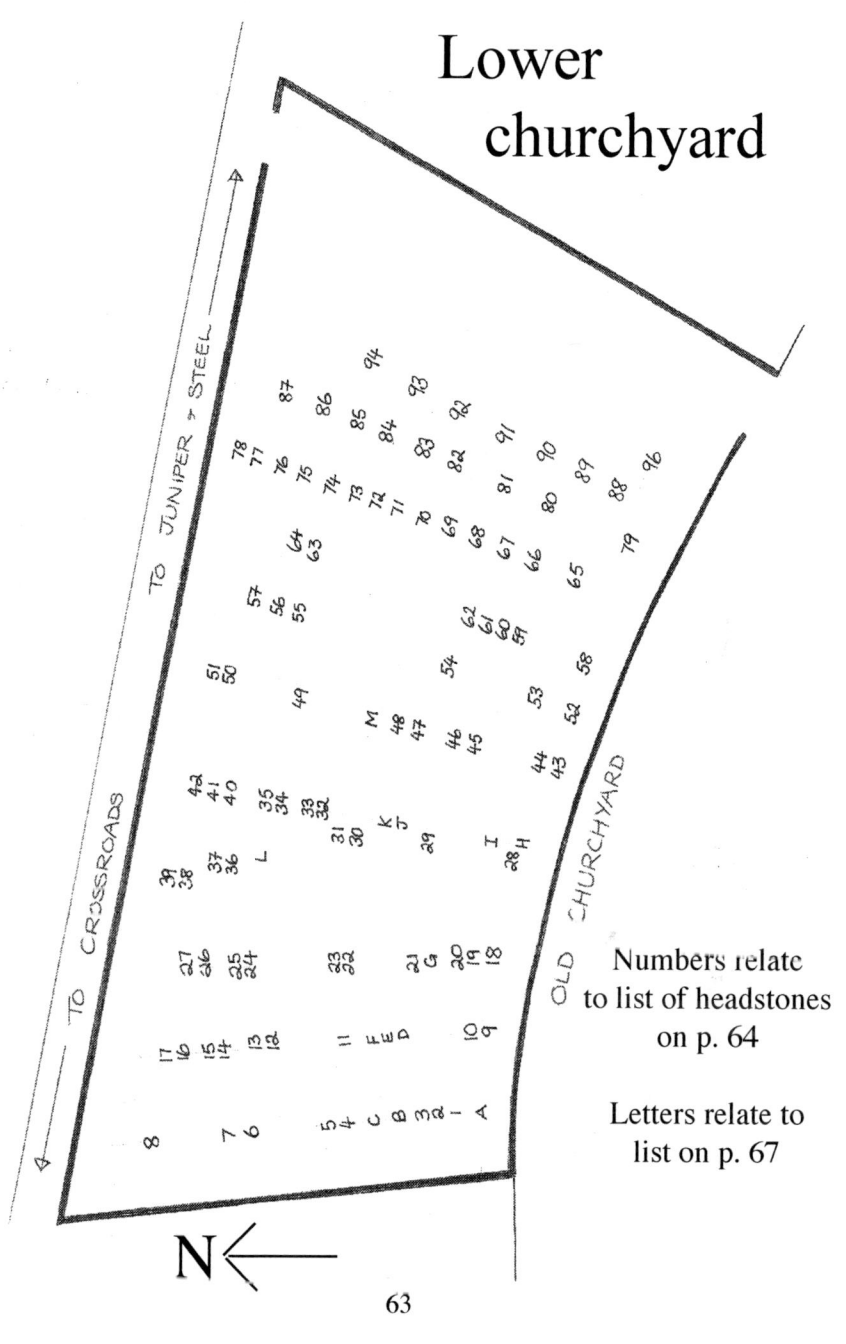

Numbers relate to list of headstones on p. 64

Letters relate to list on p. 67

CHAPTER 5

HEADSTONES
IN 'NEW' LOWER CHURCHYARD

		Burial
1.	DODD Hannah	18.9.1951
2.	ROBSON Ann C.	6.1.1972
3.	ROBSON Cuthbert	5.2.1959
4.	STEEL Jane	3.3.1957
5.	STEEL Thomas	22.12.1950
6.	NICHOL Hannah A.	7.10.1992
7.	NICHOL Joseph	30.12.1952
8.	CARR Thomas G.	9.4.1953
9.	NICHOL N. Alice	18.12.1983
10.	NICHOL Tom	30.4.1955
11.	ARMSTRONG John R.	10.9.1954
12.	ARMSTRONG Florence	26.5.1995
13.	ARMSTRONG John T.	23.5.1994
14.	HALL Robert	31.12.1963
15.	HALL Jane	12.1.1986
16.	PIGG Margaret	7.4.1978
17.	PIGG Joseph H.	11.2.1956
18.	TURNBULL Ella	27.1.2003
19.	THORBURN John	24.3.1958
20.	STEPHENSON Lillian V.	11.7.1970
21.	STEPHENSON William H.	12.12.1958
22.	GAZZANI Elizabeth	24.1.1959
23.	CLARK Margaret I.	26.2.1988
24.	CLARK Joe	22.8.1959
25.	BERECZ Maria	12.4.1984
26.	BERECZ Mimaly	3.5.1960
27.	CARR Margaret	6.1.1971
28.	CARR George	5.10.1960
29.	MAKEPEACE Whitfield	6.4.1961
30.	ROBSON Cuthbert H.	13.12.1961
31.	HAMILTON Annie	22.1.1966
32.	HAMILTON James	10.9.1964

33.	KENNEDY Olive	14.5.1970
34.	KENNEDY John	26.8.1968
35.	HENDERSON Violet	8.10.1996
36.	HENDERSON Joseph W.	9.5.1970
37.	COWING Ada	5.8.1993
38.	COWING Matthew C.	16.1.1965
39.	SIMPSON ? A.	4.8.1967
40.	SIMPSON Harry G.	15.7.1965
41.	PURVIS Margaret E.	29.12.1993
42.	PURVIS Thomas W.	29.12.1979
43.	PURVIS Robert	31.1.1972
44.	CARR Louisa	3.1.1976
45.	CARR Joseph F.	13.1.1966
46.	SNAITH Hannah	31.12.1975
47.	SNAITH Michael	26.7.1984
48.	PURVIS Ruth M.	20.1.1987
49.	PURVIS Albert	8.3.1976
50.	WILSON Vera	11.8.1978
51.	KENNEDY Katherine	5.11.1987
52.	KENNEDY Robert R.	20.9.1983
53.	SCOTT Elizabeth E.	24.12.1982
54.	DODD Thomas W.	25.2.1983
55.	ROBSON James R.	8.7.1981
56.	ORD Richard F.	27.2.1984
57.	DINNING John T.	17.11.1983
58.	ELLERINGTON David	5.5.1983
59.	MACKENZIE Hilda	16.8.1985
60.	COMMON Ann	7.2.1986
61.	STOBBS Annie E.	2.7.2001
62.	STOBBS Edward	31.10.1986
63.	CLARK Matthew	21.1.1993
64.	FORSTER William	1.4.1989
65.	HUDSPITH John I.	24.11.1987
66.	SWANEPOEL Dina J.	7.7.1990
67.	McKINNON Mary	22.9.1990
68.	TAILFORD Gordon	7.11.1990
69.	KENNEDY William	2.7.1993
70.	KOBBS Oliver A.	13.8.1993

71. CHALMERS Freda   14.1.1994
72. FOSTER George   27.5.1994
73. RUTHERFORD Mary   4.7.1994
74. DODWELL Philippa J.   22.10.1994
75. REED John   11.3.1993
76. REED John A.   24.3.1990
77. ROBB Ann G.   16.11.1989
78. CAPES Margaret J.   7.8.2000
79. CAPES Douglas E.   4.11.1989
80. CARTER Philip J.   18.10.1995
81. WHITE Stuart   7.3.1996
82. TRIFFIT Audrey M.   5.9.1996
83. PICKWORTH Arthur J.   4.11.1997
84. JOHNSON Peter L.   22.1.1999
85. HARDING Edward   19.10.2001
86. DINNING Arthur   11.3.2002
87. SWALLOW B. Alan   19.12.2002
88. SWANEPOEL Christo F.   4.12.1997
89. HESLOP George C.   21.1.1999
90. MARSH Sarah E.G.   25.9.1999
91. SPARKE M. Cyril   11.2.2002
92. MILBURN G. Walter   22.11.2000
93. BURN Edward E.   14.2.2001
94. CASSON Carolina   4.7.2002
95. MOULD Harold   11.10.2002
96. WHITE Clarence   7.1.2003

CHAPTER 6

UNMARKED BURIALS IN LOWER CHURCHYARD
(possible locations)

A.	LANGSTAFF Jessie Ann	63	1.12.1950
B.	ROBSON Annie May	48	12.10.1950
C.	ROBSON William	69	28.5.1958
D.	WILSON Robt. Frederick	51	11.2.1953
E.	JEWITT Henry	54	16.5.1959
F.	PURVIS Fred	65	11.5.1953
G.	RODDAM William	79	28.7.1956
H.	MAKEPEACE Eleanor	78	31.12.1971
I.	MAUGHAN George	84	7.9.1961
J.	DODD Mable Moore	67	12.3.1962
K.	DODD Norman Anthony	69	12.1.1962
L.	DODD Amy Isobel	67	12.1.1965
M.	ROBSON William	69	22.9.1976

Let us now praise famous men and our fathers that begat us...
There be of them that have left a name behind them,
that their praises might be reported
And some there be which have no memorial; who are perished,
as though they had never been; and are become as though they had never been born;
and their childen after them.
But these were merciful men, whose righteousness hath not been forgotten.
With their seed shall continually remain a good inheritance,
and their childen are within the covenant.
Their seed standeth fast, and their children for their sakes.
Their seed shall remain for ever and their glory shall not be blotted out.
Their bodies are buried in peace; but their name liveth for evermore.

Ecclesiastes x/1v

BURIALS IN LOWER CHURCHYARD
(locations unknown)

HALL Margaret Helen	1year	1.8.1950
HALL Susan Janette	5mths	26.6.1952
HENDERSON Margaret	77	18.2.1953
DAVISON Herbert	59	29.4.1953
BOWMAN Margaret Annie	67	28.12.53
BELL Mary	54	30.7.1954
NICHOL Annie	82	20.1.1954
MAUGHAN Helen Johnstone	84	21.2.1955
REDSHAW James William	75	25.3.1955
DIXON Margaret Jane	75	11.4.1956
NIXON Mary Elizabeth	70	21.7.1958
WADDILOVE Geo.Ed.Darley	73	5.8.1958
BELL Phillip	60	15.4.1959
REAY Mary	82	12.4.1960
CARR William	71	10.10.1960
LOADMAN May	83	26.1.1961
CORBY Bruce	64	11.9.1963
SNOWDON Edward	65	1.11.1963
HESLOP Hannah	89	2.3.1964
HALL Charles	77	2.3.1964
ARNOLD Elizabeth Durham	72	13.12.1966
ARNOLD Paige Connoly	69	20.3.1967
ROBSON Mary	5days	11.10.1967
BATY Eva Mildred	88	27.12.1968
ELLIOTT John Peter	85	10.4.1971
FORSTER Robert	74	23.11.1971
HETHERINGTON Evelyn	62	26.4.1973
SNAITH William	55	10.5.1973
CARR Joseph James	86	18.5.1977
HERDMAN Maud Robson	52	19.7.1979
HETHERINGTON Geo. Bewick	73	26.11.1979